Journal of
MEDIA ECONOMICS

Volume 15, Number 3   2002

SPECIAL ISSUE ON THE ECONOMICS OF THE MULTICHANNEL VIDEO PROGRAM DISTRIBUTION INDUSTRY

T0347282

CONTRIBUTORS

Sylvia M. Chan-Olmsted is an associate professor in the Department of Telecommunication, College of Journalism and Communications, University of Florida, Gainesville, FL 32611.

Myung-Hyun Kang is an assistant professor in the School of Communication at Hallym University in Kangwon-do, Korea 200-702.

Jack C. C. Li is an assistant professor in the Department of Telecommunication at National Chung Cheng University in Taiwan, R.O.C.

Ronald J. Rizzuto is a professor in the Reiman School of Finance, Daniels College of Business, University of Denver, Denver, CO 80210.

Michael O. Wirth is professor and chair of the Department of Mass Communications & Journalism Studies and director of the School of Communication at the University of Denver, Denver, CO 80208.

Michael Zhaoxu Yan is an assistant professor in the Department of Communication Studies at the University of Michagan, Ann Arbor, MI 48109.

JOURNAL OF MEDIA ECONOMICS, *15*(3), 151–152

INTRODUCTION

Economics of the Multichannel Video Program Distribution Industry

Michael O. Wirth
Department of Mass Communications and Journalism Studies
School of Communication
University of Denver

The multichannel video program distribution (MVPD) industry began in Lansford, Pennsylvania, in 1949 to 1950 when Robert Tarlton built a master antenna on top of the Allegheny Mountains near Summit Hill, Pennsylvania. This allowed Tarlton to retransmit Philadelphia television stations via coaxial cable to Lansford subscribers willing to pay a $125 installation fee and $3 per month for community antenna television service (Baldwin & McVoy, 1988).

In the 50-plus years that have elapsed since these humble beginnings, the MVPD industry has grown to dominate video delivery in the United States. As of June 2001, the Federal Communications Commission (FCC) reported that there are 88.3 million MVPD households in the United States (86.4% of U.S. TV households; FCC, 2001). Cable's share of the MVPD market stands at 78%, with almost 69 million subscribers, whereas the share of direct broadcast satellite (DBS) entrepreneurs (i.e., DirecTV and EchoStar) has increased to 18%, with more than 16 million subscribers (FCC, 2001). Likewise, the FCC reports that there are 294 national satellite-delivered program services competing for MVPD distribution.

Over the last decade, the MVPD industry has become increasingly complex as a result of technological innovation (e.g., digital signal compression, the Internet, etc.), increased competition (particularly from DBS), government deregulation and reregulation, and evolving consumer tastes with respect to choice, control,

Requests for reprints should be sent to Michael O. Wirth, Department of Mass Communications and Journalism Studies, School of Communication, University of Denver, Denver, CO 80208. E-mail: mwirth@du.edu convenience, cost, and community. MVPD entrepreneurs participate in an increasingly diverse marketplace in which winners and losers are determined by (a) decisions to make (or not to make) high-risk investments in new products made possible by technological innovation, (b) "speed-to-market" decisions with respect to new product innovations, (c) decisions on how to market new products to consumers, and (d) government regulation.

The dominant position of the MVPD industry coupled with its increasing complexity prompted the decision to put together this special issue of the *Journal of Media Economics,* which contains four articles that focus on a number of important MVPD market issues and concerns.

In this issue, Sylvia Chan-Olmsted and Jack Li employ strategic groups management theory and cluster analysis to empirically identify a number of MVPD programmer strategic groups. They also assess the relation between membership in a strategic MVPD programmer group and financial performance.

Michael Zhaoxu Yan uses a unique historical U. S. General Accounting Office data set and count models to empirically examine the factors affecting cable operators' local television station carriage decisions in 1989, a period in which the FCC had no must carry rules in place. The analysis focuses on the impact of cable operator horizontal concentration and vertical integration on local station carriage.

Myung-Hyun Kang utilizes diffusion theory and discriminant analysis to dissect the key factors determining whether consumers become early adopters of digital cable. He also identifies the key factors related to the speed of consumer adoption of cable's principle competitive response to DBS competition (i.e., digital cable).

Ronald Rizzuto and Michael Wirth lay out the basic economic and technological assumptions underlying cable operators' attempts to use their digital platforms to deliver "on-demand" video services. They use simulation analysis and sensitivity analysis to identify the factors most likely to determine the economic viability of video on demand.

Although much territory is left to explore, I hope that readers will find this special issue of the *Journal of Media Economics* a valuable resource in expanding their understanding of the MVPD industry. In closing, I express my thanks to my wife, Alice, for her support and understanding; to the authors of the articles for their excellent work; and to Alan Albarran for his help and guidance throughout the process of putting together this special issue.

REFERENCES

Baldwin, T. F., & McVoy, D. S. (1988). *Cable communication* (2nd ed.). Englewood Cliffs, NJ: Prentice Hall.

Federal Communications Commission. (2001, December 27). *Eighth annual report: In the matter of annual assessment of competition in the market for the delivery of video programming* [CS Docket No. 01–129]. Retrieved January 21, 2002, from http://www.fcc.gov/mb/csrptpg.html

JOURNAL OF MEDIA ECONOMICS, *15*(3), 153–174

Strategic Competition in the Multichannel Video Programming Market: An Intraindustry Strategic Group Study of Cable Programming Networks

Sylvia M. Chan-Olmsted
Department of Telecommunication
College of Journalism and Communications
University of Florida

Jack C. C. Li
Department of Telecommunication
National Chung Cheng University, Taiwan, R.O.C.

This study applied a strategic management theory—strategic groups—to assess the strategic patterns of multichannel video programmers and the relation between group membership and performance. Seven strategic groups were identified using grouping variables such as size, vertical integration, operating efficiency, differentiation, and pricing. There appears to be a relation between group membership and financial performance in this market. It is interesting to note that the results indicate neither size nor vertical integration was related to a programmer's financial performance.

The number of subscribers to both cable TV and noncable multichannel video programming distributor (MVPD) services has grown to reach over 80 million U.S. households (Federal Communications Commission [FCC], 1999b). Likewise, the landscape of the video programming industry continues to change rapidly. With the development of alternative MVPD services and the arrival of digital television, the strategic importance of content—the product for distribution—is amplified. As the role of multichannel video programmers such as CNN and ESPN becomes

Requests for reprints should be sent to Sylvia M. Chan-Olmsted, Department of Telecommunication, College of Journalism and Communications, University of Florida, Gainesville, FL 32611. E-mail: chanolmsted@jou.ufl.edu more significant with competing MVPD services, an assessment of the strategic patterns employed by these video programmers is critical to our understanding of the emerging MVPD industry.

Past economic discussions of the broadcast television industry have assumed that all programming distributors in the market use the same funding mechanism and deliver products to a fairly homogeneous group of buyers. Such a presumption does not apply to MVPD market programmers. For example, whereas CNN charges MVPDs (i.e., cable and direct broadcast satellite [DBS]) a fairly high license fee to carry its signals, many new start-up multichannel video programmers provide MVPDs with incentives to induce carriage. USA Network carries commercials, whereas the Independent Film Channel does not offer any local or national avails (i.e., commercial spots). Furthermore, multichannel video programmers often offer differentiated programming products, and the buyers may deliver these products via different distribution platforms. In essence, the traditional emphasis on industry as a unit of analysis is not appropriate for analysis of these heterogeneous programmers. In this article, we apply a strategic management theory—strategic groups—to assess the strategic patterns of multichannel video programmers and the relation between group membership and performance.

MULTICHANNEL STRATEGIC GROUP COMPETITION MODEL

Because of the capacity of multiple communication channels, firms in the MVPD industry operate under a more complex business system than the traditional broadcast industry and thus are capable of more diverse strategic competition. The observation that strategic diversity within an industry has a significant bearing on market behavior is central to the theory of strategic groups and grounds this study. The MVPD industry is inherently heterogeneous, as MVPD programmers may be supported by advertisers or subscribers or both, have the capacity to offer general appeal as well as specialized programs, and may utilize different MVPD delivery technologies.

Porter (1985; see also Cool, 1985) defined a *strategic group* as a cluster of firms that follow similar strategies in terms of the key decision variables. Firms within a strategic group resemble one another closely, recognize their mutual dependence, and thus coordinate their behavior effectively. Furthermore, when one considers intergroup market dynamics, the existence of different strategic groups affects the overall level of rivalry in the industry. When firms are associated with different strategic groups, they have different preferences about pricing, research and development, advertising, optimal output, and other market conduct. As a consequence, operational differences complicate the process of cooperation (either explicit or implicit) between groups (McGee, 1985). Hence, groups with similar strategic approaches are more likely to cooperate than groups that use diverse strategies. Moreover, cooperation is easier and more likely to happen within groups than between groups. Also, environmental changes do not have equal impact on different strategic groups due to the groups' different strategic postures, assets, and skills.

As for the performance differences among strategic group members, many strategic group scholars have argued that there are group-specific entry barriers (i.e., mobility barriers) that provide protection to group members (Mascarenhas & Aaker, 1989; Olusoga, Mokwa, & Noble, 1995). Such structural forces impede firms from freely changing their competitive positions and explain intraindustry profit differentials in a cross-section of industries (Caves & Ghemawat, 1992). Incorporating the strategic groups concept, Chan-Olmsted (1997) proposed that the multichannel video programming market would, by its heterogeneous nature, exhibit monopolistically competitive market behavior at the industry level. In other words, these firms attempt to build differential advantages (e.g., programming differentiation) and selectively interact with certain competitors' strategic actions. To rationalize such selective competitive behavior and at the same time provide a more systematic framework for studying firm strategy, Chan-Olmsted (1997) suggested moving away from simply using industry as a unit of analysis in the study of MVPD programmers' market strategy. Instead, these firms should be examined at both an industry level and in a group setting with expectations of oligopolistic market behavior—namely, recognition of mutual dependency (i.e., taking one another's changes into consideration and realizing that any change in conduct causes strategic responses from competitors). The proposed model also asserts that the relative size of MVPD firms within a group influences the degree of mutual dependence among the firms. The more equal the relative size between programmers, the more attention is paid to the interdependence. If a multichannel strategic group is comprised of a few programmers that are unequal in size, the smaller firms' strategic actions have less of an impact and thus are taken less seriously by larger firms.

As for intergroup competition, the multichannel video programming industry is hypothesized to consist of a number of strategic groups that are influenced by a number of factors affecting the competitive intensity and pattern between different strategic groups in the market. The proposed theory suggests that the strategic distance between groups and the number and size distribution of groups will affect the intensity of industry competition. For example, if MVPD programmers in various groups choose to engage in diverse strategic activities such as very different programming approaches, overall industry competitiveness should become less intensive because these groups are geographically separate in the marketplace. By selecting different niches, these strategic groups avoid any unnecessary competitive behavior and prosper together by sharing the environment. On the other hand, if the groups are close to each other with no definite and clear boundaries (e.g., similar programming), encroachment occurs, and to survive, fierce competition may result as groups defend their strategic territories. Likewise, if the size of strategic groups is distributed un-evenly, the competition may be more active because larger strategic group configu-rations tend to be unstable as less successful MVPD programmers in the group try to become more competitive by altering their market strategies to obtain differential advantages. This may gradually lead them into a different group. Also, as the number of strategic groups increases, the probability of strategic territory encroachment in-creases, potentially intensifying intergroup competition.

As discussed earlier, the economic notion of mobility barriers explains the structural and behavioral forces that keep potential entrants from easily entering a certain strategic group and eroding the group profits. Chan-Olmsted (1997) argued that multichannel programmers, who choose and operationally execute successful approaches in the key strategic dimensions, are not easily imitated by other pro-gram distributors because of the insulation created by their mobility barriers. Stra-tegic groups that possess high mobility barriers are expected to be relatively more insulated from competition and to have superior bargaining power with both ex-hibitors and producers.

MULTICHANNEL VIDEO PROGRAMMING MARKET

Cable TV continues to be the dominant distribution system for multichannel video programming, serving 82% of MVPD subscribers in 1999 with its increasing delivery capacity (FCC, 1999b). The most significant MVPD competitor to cable is DBS, which represents 12.5% of all MVPD subscribers. DBS entrepreneurs have higher lev-els of consumer satisfaction and lower average monthly programming prices com-pared to cable (FCC, 1999b). With the passage of the Satellite Home Viewer Improve-ment Act of 1999 (FCC, 1999a), DBS has become a more viable MVPD competitor. Nevertheless, DBS service providers continue to comment that access to vertically in-tegrated cable programming networks is still a significant competitive barrier.

To protect their position in this media market, multichannel video programmers continue to invest heavily in the development of their products, pouring over $7 billion into programming in 2001 (Cable Advertising Bureau, 2001). New niche multichannel video networks from Baby TV to the Wedding Channel continue to emerge. In fact, as the multichannel space becomes more populated, most new pro-grammers shy away from broad-appeal programming lineups. Instead, product dif-ferentiation and audience segmentation have become the strategic market norm. As a result, the number of subscribers reached by MVPD programmers varies tre-mendously (e.g., Discovery Channel is delivered to over 78 million subscribers, and Oxygen is available to less than 10 million households; FCC, 1999a). Al-though audiences are able to enjoy a greater number of programming choices, the proliferation of programming suppliers signals a more competitive marketplace for multichannel video programmers. At the same time, the increasing availability of noncable MVPD systems elevates the importance of strategic planning in the marketing of these programming products.

Approximately 18% of MVPD programmers are premium channels that generate their revenues from subscription fees without advertiser support. The revenue growth for these premium channels has been modest. On the other hand, the advertiser-supported programmers have seen a 140% increase in advertising revenues from 1996 to 2001, reaching $12 billion in advertising revenues for network cable in 2001 (Cable Advertising Bureau, 2001). The increasing reliance on advertising revenues for these programmers amplifies the importance of strategies in attracting audiences and the gate-keeping role of the delivery systems in controlling the programmers' access to audiences.

Amidst the recent waves of mergers and acquisitions in the media industries, the level of concentration in the national market for the buyers of multichannel video programming has actually decreased according to the FCC (1999b). The overall Herhindahl-Hirschman Index for cable system operators declined from 1,013 in 1996 to 923 in 1999 (FCC, 1999a). The combined market shares of the top 4 multiple system operators (MSOs) remained relatively stable at about 53% to 54%, whereas the top 10 MSO figures increased slightly from 71% to 75% during the same period. In essence, the buyer's market power, as one of the factors that affect competition in an industry (Porter, 1985), has remained steady in the multichannel video programming market.

RESEARCH DESIGN AND VARIABLE OPERATIONALIZATION

The following research questions guided this study:

1. What different strategic groups are there in the multichannel video programming market?
2. What is the relation between strategic group membership and performance in the multichannel video programming market?
3. What strategic positions deliver superior performance in this market?

Most strategic groups studies have subscribed to the notion that strategic group formation should be based on scope and resource commitment variables,[1] the strategic dimensions that are key to gaining and maintaining competitive advantage in

---

[1]*Core scope variables* are operational strategies such as market segments targeted, types of products or services offered in the market (differentiation), research and development, pricing, and advertising. *Resource variables* are more established beneficial strategic positions such as efficiency, size, and years of operation.

target product–market segments (Fiegenbaum & Thomas, 1995; Olusoga et al., 1995). We propose that the core scope and resource variables most likely to create competitive advantages in the MVPD programming market are size, vertical integration, horizontal integration, history, operating efficiency, product differentiation, programming development, pricing, advertising product availability, and degree of reliance on multiple revenue streams.

Multichannel Video Programmer Size

As noted by Cool and Schendel (1987), firm size influences the ability to allocate different amounts of resources to different functional areas. Firm size is one of the most frequently used variables for identifying strategic groups in various industries (Cool & Dierickx, 1993; Fiegenbaum & Thomas, 1995; Olusoga et al., 1995; Veliyath & Ferris, 1997). A resource-based variable, potential market size is particularly critical in the media market because media products have the nature of public goods. Therefore, any subsequent new viewer added to the existing customer base will increase profits. The size of an MVPD programmer (i.e., its number of subscribers) has significant implications for its subscriber revenues, advertising revenue potential (if any), power to negotiate with system operators, and ability to invest in original programming as well as new technology.

Vertical Integration With System Operators

MVPD system operators and program distributors have a symbiotic relation: The delivery systems need an ample supply of programming to attract and retain subscribers, and video programmers need access to subscribers to compete. Economic necessities have led cable operators and networks to integrate vertically (Owen & Wildman, 1992). Klein (1989) found that vertically integrated MSOs were more likely to carry a cable network in which they had an ownership interest. Nevertheless, these MSOs were also more likely than nonvertically integrated MSOs to carry networks in which they had no financial interest. Waterman and Weiss (1997) suggested that cable networks could benefit from their vertically integrated relation with cable systems, especially major MSOs such as Time Warner and Cox. It was concluded that although the relation between a cable system and a cable network can be based on simple contractual agreement, an ownership relation would likely facilitate the contracting process. Furthermore, a cable operator with financial interest in a programming supplier has a greater incentive to assign the network a more favorable channel position and to provide additional program promotions. Nevertheless, Crandall (1990) found no statistically significant difference between vertically integrated MSOs and nonvertically integrated MSOs with respect to their network carriage decisions. Because most studies have revealed some degree of competitive advantage derived from the integration with MVPD buyers, the *vertical integration* strategic dimension was included in the grouping process and is defined as the number of subscribers reached by the MSOs owned by the same parent company or companies. (Partial ownership was adjusted accordingly.)

Horizontal Integration With Other Video Programmers

The ownership of multiple MVPD programming services is becoming more common as many established multichannel programmers branch into subniche network territory. For example, BET started a BET on Jazz network, and Discovery Channel introduced sister networks such as Discovery People and Animal Planet. The benefits of being affiliated with various MVPD programmers include such possibilities as cost-cutting from the sharing of resources and talent; the ability to offer advertisers innovative, targeted advertising packages; and the ability to pre-empt competition by saturating a programming niche. *Horizontal integration,* defined as the number of other cable or broadcast TV networks that are owned by the same parent company or companies, can also enhance the bargaining power of networks against advertisers as well as system operators.

History and Operating Efficiency

Multichannel programmers such as CNN, Nickelodeon, and MTV, which have a long history of operation, are often regarded as the foundation networks on cable systems (Eastman, 1997). Such a "first-comer" status has led to higher license fees and advertising revenues for the more established networks. The *history variable* is defined as the number of months a cable program network has been in operation from its launch through the end of 1998.

Veliyath & Ferris (1997), in their study of mobility barriers, found efficiency to be an important strategic factor that often affects a strategic group's financial performance. To take into account a video programmer's ability to efficiently apply its resources in nonprogramming areas, an *operating efficiency variable,* defined as total selling, general, and administrative expenses[2] as a percentage of total net revenue, was included in the group formation procedure.

Product Differentiation

A scope-oriented variable, product differentiation is a central strategy in the multichannel video programming market. As MVPD continues to develop as a narrow-

---

[2]This is the sum of all selling, general, and administrative expenses: total overhead costs related to a basic cable network excluding expenses that can be directly attributed to actual production and programming.

casting medium, the ability to differentiate its product is critical to the success of an MVPD programmer. Bae (1999) suggested that although cable networks do not directly compete with each other, program differentiation exists among the competing cable all-news networks because each cable news network offers a distinctive program format and content approach. Many strategic groups scholars such as Veliyath & Ferris (1997) have used differentiation as one grouping strategy. To measure product differentiation, we used both a programmer's content type (children, news/information, sports, general/superstation, movies, music, religion, ethnic, educational, specific topic mix, lifestyle/leisure) and the degree of target appeal (e.g., mass = 1, niche = 2, subniche = 3). Whereas a mass category indicates a more general programming appeal targeted at a wide variety of audience, the niche category signals a somewhat narrowcasting programming approach targeted at an audience subset. Subniche networks are programming services that focus on providing the most defined type of programming. They appeal to an even smaller audience subset. For example, USA Network is in the mass category, with ESPN in the niche category and The Golf Channel in the subniche category.

Programming Development

An important development of the MVPD industry is that the programming market is no longer a key "aftermarket" for movies and off-broadcast network programs: It has become a "foremarket" in which some cable networks produce their own programs and even sell the programs back to broadcast TV (Brooks, 1997). Because the ability to develop attractive original programming has become a critical strategy for many MVPD programmers, *programming development,* a scope-based variable defined as total programming expenses as a percentage of total net revenue, was included in the group formation procedure.

Pricing[3]

Another scope-strategic variable, *pricing* (i.e., the license fee per subscriber per month), was also used to identify strategic groups (Galbraith, Merrill, & Morgan, 1994; Olusoga et al., 1995). In the MVPD programming market, pricing strategies may be used in determining license fees charged to MVPD systems or advertising rates to advertisers or both. For example, to acquire a size competitive advantage, a programmer may opt for a lower license fee to induce or increase cable carriages. On the other hand, higher license fees directly contribute to an MVPD programmer's revenue potential.

---

[3]Because the cost per thousand pricing data were incomplete for many newer programmers in the sample, an advertising pricing measure was not used in the grouping exercise.

Advertising Product Availability and Reliance
on Multiple Revenue Streams

Whereas the offering of local advertising avails provides incentives for MVPD system carriages (Eastman, 1997), national avails influence a programmer's advertising revenue potential. Accordingly, *advertising availability,* another scope variable, was included in the grouping process and is defined as (a) the number of local avails (commercial spots) for local system operators per hour and (b) the number of national avails for national advertisers per hour.

Finally, to assess an MVPD programmer's reliance on multiple revenue streams and to compare each programmer's reliance on advertising versus licensing revenues, we included two reliance variables in the procedure: (a) *reliance on advertising revenue* (i.e., advertising revenue as a percentage of total net revenue) and (b) *reliance on license revenue* (i.e., license revenue as a percentage of total net revenue).

Performance Measurement

Strategic groups scholars have used return on sales, return on assets, return on equity, market shares, and pretax profits to measure firm performance (Cool & Dierickx, 1993; Houthoofd & Heene, 1997; Olusoga et al., 1995; Veliyath & Ferris, 1997). Nevertheless, performance measurement is a perennially thorny issue in strategic management (McGee, Thomas, & Pruett, 1995). Many have criticized the narrow terms of profitability as opposed to a broader performance view including both financial and operational measures. Caves and Ghemawat (1992) argued that in exploring profit differences between groups, pretax income should be used rather than rates of return, as chosen by many strategic management scholars, because according to economic theory firms try to maximize total economic profits rather than rates of return. McGee et al. (1995) stressed the importance of using multiple measures of performance. Thus, to evaluate the performance of MVPD programmers, in this study we used a pretax income measure of total net revenue (total gross revenue excluding advertising commissions) in addition to rate of return measures such as total net revenue per subscriber and cash flow margin. Revenue per subscriber provides a more accurate performance measure by taking into account the inherent size limit of younger, niche programmers. Cash flow margin is particularly relevant to the cable TV industry, as cash flow is used as a primary measure in valuing most cable properties. The measure of cash flow margin here is the ratio of a programmer's earnings before interest, taxes, depreciation of property/plant/equipment, and amortization of intangibles to its total net revenue.

METHOD

Most strategic group studies (Cool & Schendel, 1987; Fiegenbaum & Thomas, 1995; Mascarenhas & Aaker, 1989) have used cluster analysis to statistically group firms. Clusters of firms are developed based on their scores on a set of important strategic variables representing key competitive resources typically chosen by the researcher on the basis of industry studies, expert opinion, and judgment (Fiegenbaum, Sudharshan, & Thomas, 1990). Dillon and Mulani (1989) pointed out that the major weakness of cluster analysis is that there is no natural or objective grouping in the data. Given any data matrix, it is not difficult for numerical taxonomic methods to derive statistically significant groupings (McGee et al., 1995). Punj and Stewart (1983) also argued that clusters are "fuzzy constructs" with no clear guidelines for determining the boundaries of each segment. To cope with the artificial nature of cluster analysis, as suggested by Ketchen and Shook (1996), we carefully selected the grouping variables and interpreted the emerged clusters based on prior research and industry observations.

Because a la carte pay programming services (i.e., pay cable channels such as HBO and Pay Per View) compete under a different financing and operating system and with a different set of programmers, the subjects of this study are limited to multichannel video program networks typically offered to subscribers as part of a basic or expanded basic programming tier. The data set was derived primarily from Paul Kagan Associates, Inc. (2000) *Economics of Basic Cable Networks 2000 Databook.* Initially, data were collected for all 59 basic cable networks included in the *Databook.*[4] Twelve metric measures were used to operationalize the resources and core scope variables as discussed earlier. The 59 cable networks were also coded according to their dominant programming type.[5] The categorical variable was not included in the initial analysis because of the limitation of cluster analysis in combining metric and nonmetric data in the grouping procedure. The programming types variable was later used for cluster profiling. To examine the relation between group membership and financial performance, an analysis of variance (ANOVA) was performed on the membership variable and the three performance measures discussed earlier.

To obtain the largest and most compatible sample size, the year 1998 was chosen for a cross-sectional study.[6] A total of 45 cable network programmers were included in the final analysis; the grouping procedure necessarily ex-

---

[4]Disney Channel was included because it is often marketed as part of a basic cable tier.

[5]A video programmer is classified into the *general* programming type category if it offers a diverse, broad programming content similar to those of broadcast networks (superstations are included here, e.g., USA Network). On the other hand, if it offers programming that has a variety of formats but is still in a particular interest area (e.g., Comedy Central), it is in the *specific mix* category.

[6]1999 data were not used because advertising avails were missing for most cable networks.

cludes cases with missing data in any of the measures. Also, because the variables were measured in different units, which might give more weight to variables with large values, the data were standardized prior to the statistical analysis. A two-stage cluster analysis procedure was used. First, a hierarchical cluster analysis with squared Euclidean distance measure was used to identify the most appropriate number of clusters. Based on the rules that small agglomeration coefficients indicate a combination of fairly homogeneous clusters and the joining of two very different clusters would result in a large coefficient or a large change in the coefficient, we identified two possible cluster solutions: a three-cluster solution with 26, 4, and 15 firms in each of the clusters (coefficient increased from 23.079 to 37.377) and a seven-cluster solution with 1, 3, 12, 8, 13, 6, and 2 firms in each of the clusters (coefficient increased from 15.719 to 19.913). After a careful examination of the cluster membership and the members' values in each of the grouping variables, the seven-cluster solution was selected as most appropriate based on prior industry observations and because it created the most homogeneous clusters. A nonhierarchical procedure—K-means clustering—and a one-way ANOVA were also performed to increase the validity of solutions and to ensure that the segments were mutually discrete (Punj & Stewart, 1983).

RESULTS

Strategic Groups in the MVPD Programming Market

Seven strategic groups were identified by the cluster analysis (see Table 1). We performed an ANOVA for each independent variable to examine the variances of characteristics among groups. All measures, with the exception of programming expenses as a percentage of net revenue, were found to vary significantly from group to group (see Table 2). Note that a standard deviation for Group 1 is not available because it consists of only one member (i.e., TV Guide).

Strategic Group 1: Programming guide. Highly differentiated from all others, TV Guide is the only member in this strategic group. It seems that, as the leading provider of programming schedules and information across different media platforms, TV Guide is able to re-purpose its content for multiple distribution systems and invest the lowest percentage of its net revenue in programming among all cable networks. By nature of its content, TV Guide does not compete directly with other networks. In fact, it complements other programmers. Other strategic positions of TV Guide that may generate competitive advantages include the largest number of local avails for local cable systems, lowest license fee per subscriber, and vertical integration with the largest MSO. TV Guide also has the highest num-

TABLE 1
Cluster Group Membership and Associated Programming Types

Strategic Group	Group Members (Programming Types)	Strategy (Unit)	Strategic Positions	
			M	SD
Group 1: Programming guide (1 member)	• TV Guide (news/information)	Size (no. of subs in millions)	89.5	NA
		Vertical integration (no. subs in thousands)	6,619.0	NA
		Horizontal integration (no. of sister networks)	19.0	NA
		History (months)	131.0	NA
		Operation efficiency (%)	61.7	NA
		Product differentiation (index)	2.0	NA
		Product development (%)	9.0	NA
		Pricing ($)	0.02	NA
		Product scope (no. of local ads)	18.0	NA
		Product scope (no. of national ads)	24.0	NA
		Reliance on ad revenue (%)	60.4	NA
		Reliance on license revenue (%)	39.6	NA
Group 2: Commercial-free movie (3 members)	• American Movie Classics (movie)	Size (no. of subs in millions)	40.3	25.0
	• Independent Film Channel (movie)	Vertical integration (no. subs in thousands)	3,887.0	2,267.3
	• Turner Movie Classics (movie)	Horizontal integration (no. of sister networks)	7.0	1.0
		History (months)	92.3	67.3
		Operation efficiency (%)	42.0	10.7
		Product differentiation (index)	3.0	0.0
		Product development (%)	47.7	30.7
		Pricing ($)	0.14	0.05
		Product scope (no. of local ads)	0	0
		Product scope (no. of national ads)	0	0
		Reliance on ad revenue (%)	0	0
		Reliance on license revenue (%)	99.7	0.6
Group 3: Young, differentiated, integrated (12 members)	• Animal Planet (educational)	Size (no. of subs in millions)	36.4	16.0
	• Cartoon Network (children)	Vertical integration (no. subs in thousands)	4,612.7	2,595.7
	• CNN/fin (news/information)	Horizontal integration (no. of sister networks)	13.6	4.4
	• Comedy Central (specific mix)	History (months)	66.1	34.5

Court TV (specific mix)
E! (specific mix)
Food Network (life/leisure)
Golf Channel (sports)
History Channel (educational)
Outdoor Life (life/leisure)
Speedvision (sports)
Travel Channel (life/leisure)

Group 4: Established, general, integrated (8 members)

BET (ethnic)
CNN + Headline News (news/info)
Discovery Channel (educational)
Fox Family Channel (general)
The Learning Channel (educational)
TBS (general)
TNT (general)
USA Network (general)

Group 5: Broadcasters' differentiated branch (13 members)

A&E Network (specific mix)
Box (music)
CNBC (news/info)
Country Music TV (music)
ESPN2 (sports)
Home & Garden TV (life/leisure)
Lifetime (general)
MTV (music)
Nickelodeon (children)
Sci-Fi Channel (specific mix)
TNN (music)

Operation efficiency (%)	49.4	21.8
Product differentiation (index)	2.5	0.5
Product development (%)	80.4	52.0
Pricing ($)	0.07	0.04
Product scope (no. of local ads)	5.2	1.0
Product Scope (no. of national ads)	17.1	2.2
Reliance on ad revenue (%)	51.0	13.3
Reliance on license revenue (%)	44.4	16.9
Size (no. of subs in millions)	80.9	27.2
Vertical integration (no. subs in thousands)	4,657.0	3,002.2
Horizontal integration (no. of sister networks)	8.6	4.1
History (months)	212.4	48.1
Operation efficiency (%)	22.3	6.1
Product differentiation (index)	1.5	0.5
Product development (%)	39.5	12.2
Pricing ($)	0.22	0.15
Product scope (no. of local ads)	3.8	1.7
Product scope (no. of national ads)	16.8	4.0
Reliance on ad revenue (%)	57.5	8.9
Reliance on license revenue (%)	40.2	7.8
Size (no. of subs in millions)	62.7	13.7
Vertical integration (no. subs in thousands)	0	0
Horizontal integration (no. of sister networks)	6.2	3.5
History (months)	153.9	59.7
Operation efficiency (%)	23.8	13.3
Product differentiation (index)	2.2	0.4
Product development (%)	42.9	11.3
Pricing ($)	0.11	0.06
Product scope (no. of local ads)	4.3	0.8
Product scope (no. of national ads)	17.3	3.9
Reliance on ad revenue (%)	62.7	9.3

(continued)

TABLE 1 (Continued)

Strategic Group	Group Members (Programming Types)	Strategic Positions		
		Strategy (Unit)	M	SD
		Reliance on license revenue (%)	30.1	12.0
Group 6: Small but trying (6 members)	• VH1 (music) • Weather Channel (news/info) • Bravo (specific mix) • F/X (general) • Game Show Network (life/leisure) • Goodlife TV Network (general) • Knowledge TV (educational) • MSNBC (news/info)	Size (no. of subs in millions) Vertical integration (no. subs in thousands) Horizontal integration (no. of sister networks) History (months) Operation efficiency (%) Product differentiation (index) Product development (%) Pricing ($) Product scope (no. of local ads) Product scope (no. of national ads) Reliance on ad revenue (%) Reliance on license revenue (%)	29.2 429.7 3.7 90.3 93.1 2.2 83.3 0.11 3.8 17.5 28.3 57.3	14.4 1,052.5 4.0 83.7 68.7 0.8 85.1 0.10 2.0 2.8 14.1 13.7
Group 7: Established and content valued (2 members)	• Disney Channel (children) • ESPN (sports)	Size (no. of subs in millions) Vertical integration (no. subs in thousands) Horizontal integration (no. of sister networks) History (months) Operation efficiency (%) Product differentiation (index) Product development (%) Pricing ($) Product scope (no. of local ads) Product scope (no. of national ads) Reliance on ad revenue (%) Reliance on license revenue (%)	57.9 0 8.0 209.5 20.6 2.0 40.3 0.67 2.0 8.0 22.8 70.5	25.2 0 0.0 30.4 7.5 0.0 10.4 0.03 2.8 11.3 32.2 33.5

Note. Subs = subscriptions; NA = not applicable; ads = advertisements; ad = advertising.

TABLE 2
Analysis of Variances for Grouping Variables

Variable		Sum of Squares	df	M	F	Significance
No. of subscribers	Between	15,992.61	6	2,665.44	7.67	.00
	Within	13,206.07	38	347.53		
	Total	29,198.69	44			
Avgerage license	Between	0.71	6	0.12	16.80	.00
fee/subscription/month	Within	0.27	38	0.01		
	Total	0.98	44			
No. of MSO reach	Between	232,965,929.20	6	38,827,654.87	9.64	.00
	Within	153,024,636.00	38	4,026,964.11		
	Total	385,990,565.20	44			
No. of sister networks	Between	633.21	6	105.54	7.11	.00
	Within	564.43	38	14.85		
	Total	1,197.64	44			
No. of months in operation	Between	137,084.59	6	22,847.43	7.41	.00
	Within	117,134.21	38	3,082.48		
	Total	254,218.80	44			
SG&A/net revenue	Between	25,028.98	6	4,171.50	5.03	.00
	Within	31,512.84	38	829.29		
	Total	56,541.82	44			
Product differentiation	Between	7.05	6	1.18	4.69	.00
	Within	9.53	38	0.25		
	Total	16.58	44			
Programming expense/	Between	18,871.31	6	3,145.22	1.69	.15
net revenue	Within	70,719.95	38	1,861.05		
	Total	89,591.26	44			
No. of local advertisements	Between	266.48	6	44.41	25.28	.00
	Within	66.77	38	1.76		
	Total	333.24	44			
No. of national	Between	1,011.63	6	168.60	12.50	.00
advertisements	Within	512.69	38	13.49		
	Total	1,524.31	44			
Advertising revenue/	Between	14,307.96	6	2,384.66	16.33	.00
net revenue	Within	5,549.26	38	146.03		
	Total	19,857.22	44			
License revenue/	Between	14,221.66	6	2,370.28	12.28	.00
net revenue	Within	7,331.95	38	192.95		
	Total	21,553.61	44			

Note. MSO = multiple system operators; SG&A = selling, general, and administrative expense.

ber of sister networks. Being the only member in a strategic group, TV Guide has no within-group competition. It also holds the most distant position from all other groups based on the strategic measures. Nevertheless, these strategic advantages did not translate into financial success. Earning $58 million in net revenue, $0.65 of net revenue per subscriber, and 29.3% cash flow margin, TV Guide exhibited the worst financial performance among all groups.

Strategic Group 2: Commercial-free movie programmers.   This is the most content homogeneous strategic group. All three members here offer movie products commercial free and rely on license fees as their primary revenue source. An examination of the ownership shows some interesting patterns. Both American Movie Classics (AMC) and the Independent Film Channel are co-owned by a major MSO, Cablevision (75%) and NBC (25%). Accordingly, the two movie channels are strategically differentiated: AMC offers classic, general-appeal Hollywood movies, and the Independent Film Channel provides newer, narrow-appeal films. Competing against AMC, Turner Classic Movies (TCM) is also vertically integrated with one of the leading MSOs, AOL Time Warner. Although AMC has the first-comer advantage in this group with twice as many subscribers, TCM has access to AOL Time Warner's studio products and film libraries. Though all three networks offer movie products, an oligopolistic, interdependent relation seems to exist in this cluster. TCM and AMC priced their products (AMC at $0.19 per subscriber per month; TCM at $0.15 per subscriber per month) comparably and spent similar proportions of their net revenues on programming (AMC, 29.1%; TCM, 30.9%), whereas the Independent Film Channel is content differentiated and thus not in direct competition with the other two. Firms in this group generated only modest net revenue ($73 million) and net revenue per subscriber ($1.53) and achieved the lowest cash flow margin (29.1%).

Strategic Group 3: Young, differentiated, and integrated programmers.
This group consists of 12 cable networks with a diverse programming content mix. Eleven of the 12 networks are affiliated with MSOs and all members have many affiliated programming networks (M = 13.6; see Table 1). This group also consists predominantly of younger networks (M = 66.1 months). It seems that most of these networks emerged in the early 1990s as the second wave of niche programming after the cable industry experienced the success of the original niche networks such as ESPN and MTV. To establish a differentiated position, members of this group try to provide even more defined programming content, spending over 80% of their net revenues on programming. Perhaps due to newness, this group had the second lowest average license fee ($0.07 per subscriber per month) and a relatively small subscriber base (36 million), operating in modest efficiency (49.4%). Firms in the group generated very modest net revenue ($67 million net revenue and $1.72 of net

revenue per subscriber), but they achieved a relatively high cash flow margin (49.7%).

Strategic Group 4: Established, general, and integrated programmers. This is the most established strategic group with eight cable networks that were early market entrants (many have been in operation for more than 20 years). Seven of the eight networks here are owned by top MSOs such as AT&T, AOL Time Warner, and Cox. This group has the largest number of subscribers when TV Guide is excluded ($M = 80.9$ million), it is very efficient ($M = 22.3\%$), and it demands the second highest license fee per subscriber ($M = \$0.22$ per subscriber per month). An examination of program content and audience appeal reveals some patterns. Half of the group members (i.e., Fox Family, TBS, TNT, and USA Network) offer general-appeal programming. Although CNN and Headline News provide news/information, their content is at the general end of the spectrum in this content category. The same holds true for networks like BET and Discovery Channel. To a certain extent, this group may be characterized as the cablecasters' broadcast tier. This is the second best performing group in terms of net revenue ($500 million) and net revenue per subscriber ($6.21). It achieves a cash flow margin of 38.2%.

Strategic Group 5: Broadcasters' differentiated cable programmers. Group 5 may be characterized as the over-the-air broadcasters' strategic cable tier. This group has the largest number of networks (13). Except for the Weather Channel and HGTV, these networks are owned by CBS/Viacom, NBC, or ABC/Disney. It is interesting that none of these networks is affiliated with an MSO. This group contains the largest cluster of music programmers (5). Similar to their broadcast parent companies, firms in the group rely mostly on advertising revenues ($M = 62.7\%$). They also did not command very high license fees ($M = \$0.11$ per subscriber per month) and received only about 30% of their net revenue from this source. This strategic group seems to deliver narrowcasting, niche programming opportunities for broadcasters. The financial performance of the group was modest with $284 million total net revenue, $4.02 of net revenue per subscriber, and a cash flow margin of 36.4%.

Strategic Group 6: Small but trying programmers. This group consists of six networks with very diverse history, content, size, operating efficiency, pricing, and degree of integration. In general, these video programmers have the smallest number of subscribers (29.2 million), the least affiliations with MSOs (with the exception of Bravo), the lowest level of horizontal affiliations (3.7 networks), and understandably the least efficient networks considering their small subscriber reach. However, they have heavily invested in product development, spending over 80% of their net revenue on programming. Relying mostly on license fee revenue, firms in this group produced less than $2.00 of net revenue per subscriber and delivered the second lowest total net revenue ($66 million). Nevertheless, these programmers were able to generate the highest rate of return, delivering a cash flow margin of 89.6%.

Strategic Group 7: Established and content-valued programmers. This group is composed of two networks, both of which are owned by ABC/Disney. These two networks are not affiliated with any MSOs. However, because of their well-established credibility (at least 15 years in operation) and highly valued content in two profitable programming segments (children and sports), they were able to charge the highest license fees among all groups ($0.67 per subscriber per month) and rely heavily on their license fee revenues (70.5%). Armed with the most efficient operation (20.6%), firms in this group have exhibited the best overall financial performance among all groups, generating $832.1 million in total net revenue, $13.50 of net revenue per subscriber, and a cash flow margin of 39.2%.

Programming types and strategic distance between groups. To take the categorical variable programming types into consideration, a cross-tab analysis was performed. The resulting chi-square test indicated that the seven strategic groups have applied significantly different programming strategies ($p < .00$). The cross-tab analysis also revealed that Group 3 has the most diverse, evenly distributed programming niches, followed by Groups 5 and 6. Only Groups 4 and 5 have four or more programmers competing in the same programming categories. Even so, these programmers do not really encroach on one another's product territory because they often further differentiate their programming emphasis (e.g., music networks MTV vs. TNN).

To examine the strategic position of each group, the Euclidean distance between each pair of clusters was measured. The values indicate the degree of similarity or dissimilarity between the clusters. With all variables taken into consideration, Group 1, the programming guide, occupies a position most dissimilar to other groups, with distances ranging from 5.6 to 9.3. The commercial-free movie group (Group 2) and the established, content-valued group (Group 7) also have a considerable degree of dissimilarity relative to other groups, with distances ranging from 4.4 to 5.8 and 4.6 to 8.9, respectively. Alternatively, Groups 3 to 6 are closer to one another, all with distance values no higher than 3.7. Overall, the pairs of Group 3 and 5, Group 3 and 6, and Group 5 and 6 occupy the closest strategic space.

Relation Between Strategic Group Membership and Performance

An ANOVA was performed to examine the correlation between group membership and performance. The statistical results, $Fs(6, 38) = 8.20$ and 9.90, respectively ($p < .05$), indicate that group membership in this market is significantly related to the total net revenue and net revenue per subscriber a video programmer generates. The relation, however, is not significant between group membership and cash flow margin, $F(6, 38) = 0.79, p > .05$.

As stated previously, Group 7 had the best total net revenue performance and Group 1 had the worst. Group 7 also delivered the highest net revenue per subscriber and Group 1 had the lowest. Although the cash flow margin variable did not show significant variance among groups, Group 6 had the highest cash flow margin and Groups 1 and 2 had the lowest.

Strategic Positions That Lead to Superior Performance

It seems that delivering niche content that is highly valued (as suggested by per subscriber license fees) by its subscribers as well as buyers (i.e., cable system operators) is the key to better financial performance for a multichannel video programmer with respect to revenues, both overall and in rate of return. It is also evident that, although higher subscriber numbers do not guarantee financial success, a long established history elevates an MVPD programmer's performance. More advertising avails and reliance on advertising revenue do not yield better margin or revenue numbers, nor does a heavy reliance on license fee revenues. Horizontal relations with other programmers and increased operating efficiency seem to contribute somewhat to the performance measures. Nevertheless, contrary to the belief of many MVPD system operators, vertical integration, although possibly enhancing carriage probability or marketing possibilities or both, is not essential for superior performance in this market. Spending a higher percentage of net revenue on programming also does not appear to lead to better overall financial outcomes.

DISCUSSION AND CONCLUSION

It is evident that MVPD programmers, in pursuit of monopolistic space (i.e., areas of natural advantage), are highly differentiated not only in their programming product but also in many of the strategic dimensions discussed. By occupying different strategic positions, most strategic groups in this market were able to carve out more definite and clear boundaries to avoid territory encroachment (i.e., direct competition).

A careful review of the group composition reveals some interesting strategic patterns. Although the presence of broadcasters may be felt through their niche cable properties in Group 5, cable-based MVPDs have tried to compete with the broadcasters with their own mass-appeal networks in Group 4. Possibly due to their longer history in operation and the higher perceived value (license fees),

Group 4 networks have outperformed Group 5, generating almost twice as much in the way of total net revenues.

Though delivering the second best overall performance in terms of within-group competition, Group 4 seems to present the highest likelihood of content encroachment among its members. The more general broadcast content model, although generating higher license fees and advertising revenues, also results in continuous pressure from other comparable programmers to deliver more high-profile or original programming product. Regarding between-group competition, Group 3 (young, differentiated, and integrated) and Group 5 (broadcasters' differentiated brand) seem to be in the most direct competition in both overall strategic distance and content appeals. As Group 3 becomes more established and the proportionately high programming investment takes effect, it may be able to demand higher license fees, deliver better advertising revenues or both, thus becoming a more competitive strategic group.

There appears to be a relation between strategic group membership and financial performance in the multichannel video programming market. It is interesting to see that, contrary to general industry belief, neither size nor vertical integration has played an important role in elevating an MVPD programmer's financial performance. The competitive advantage derived from such strategies apparently was not realized financially. Although operating efficiency and affiliation with other programmers contribute somewhat to better performance, first-comer advantage and valued content are the keys to financial success. Smaller programmers may outperform bigger programmers in rate of return when they rely mainly on license fee revenues and invest in programming to improve the value of their products.

This study is limited by its inability to include more newer cable networks, as well as CPM pricing and audience ratings to evaluate the value of a programming product from the subscribers' and advertisers' perspectives. Future research in this area may extend the strategic grouping to a multiyear analysis to examine the stability of strategic groups and their financial performance. Also, more studies are needed to investigate the environmental factors that actually influence in-group and between-group competition and to validate the proposed theoretical relation between size and strategic distance with the degree of competition in this market.

REFERENCES

Bae, H. S. (1999). Product differentiation in cable programming: The case in the cable national all-news networks. *Journal of Media Economics, 12,* 265–277.

Brooks, D. E. (1997). Basic cable network programming. In S. T. Eastman & D. A. Ferguson (Eds.), *Broadcast/cable programming: Strategies and practices* (5th ed., pp. 274–307). New York: Wadsworth.

Cable Advertising Bureau. (2001). *Media facts.* Retrieved September 5, 2001, from http://www.cabletvadbureau.com/01Facts/facts01.htm

Caves, R. E., & Ghemawat, P. (1992). Identifying mobility barriers. *Strategic Management Journal, 13,* 1–12.

Chan-Olmsted, S. M. (1997). Theorizing multichannel media economics: An exploration of a group-industry strategic competition model. *Journal of Media Economics, 10*(1), 39–49.

Cool, K. O. (1985). *Strategic group formation and strategic group shifts: A longitudinal analysis of the U.S. pharmaceutical industry, 1963–1982.* Unpublished doctoral dissertation, Purdue University, Lafayette, IN.

Cool, K., & Dierickx, I. (1993). Rivalry, strategic groups and firm profitability. *Strategic Management Journal, 14,* 47–59.

Cool, K., & Schendel, D. (1987). Performance differences among strategic group members. *Strategic Management Journal, 9,* 207–223.

Crandall, R. W. (1990). *Vertical integration and q ratios in the cable industry* [Appended to TCI reply comments]. FCC Mass Media Docket No. 89–200.

Dillon, W. R., & Mulani, N. (1989, February). LADI: A latent discriminant model for analyzing marketing research data. *Journal of Marketing Research, 26,* 15–29.

Eastman, S. T. (1997). Local cable systems and programming. In S. T. Eastman & D. A. Ferguson (Eds.), *Broadcast/cable programming: Strategies and practices* (5th ed., pp. 250–273). New York: Wadsworth.

Federal Communications Commission. (1999a). *Fact sheet of Satellite Home Viewer Improvement Act of 1999.* Retrieved June, 10, 2001, from http://www.fcc.gov/mb/shva/shviafac.doc

Federal Communications Commission. (1999b, December 30). *Sixth annual report: In the matter of annual assessment of the status of competition in markets for the delivery of video programming.* CS Docket No. 99–230.

Fiegenbaum, A., & Thomas, H. (1995). Strategic groups as reference groups: Theory, modeling and empirical examination of industry and competitive strategy. *Strategic Management Journal, 16,* 461–476.

Fiegenbaum, A., Sudharshan, D., & Thomas, H. (1990). Strategic time periods and strategic groups research: Concepts and an empirical example. *Journal of Management Studies, 27,* 133–148.

Galbraith, C. S., Merrill, G. B., & Morgan, G. (1994). Bilateral strategic groups: The market for nontactical navy information systems. *Strategic Management Journal, 15,* 613–626.

Houthoofd, N., & Heene, A. (1997). Strategic groups as subsets of strategic scope groups in the Belgian brewing industry. *Strategic Management Journal, 18,* 653–666.

Ketchen, D. J., & Shook, C. L. (1996). The application of cluster analysis in strategic management research: An analysis and critique. *Strategic Management Journal, 17,* 441–458.

Klein, B. (1989). *The competitive consequences of vertical integration in the cable industry.* Report on behalf of the National Cable Television Association, Washington, DC.

Mascarenhas, B., & Aaker, D. (1989). Mobility barriers and strategic groups. *Strategic Management Journal, 10,* 474–485.

McGee, J. (1985). Strategic groups: A bridge between industry structure and strategic management? In H. Thomas & D. Gardner (Eds.), *Strategic marketing and management* (pp. 293–313). Chichester, England: Wiley.

McGee, J., Thomas, H., & Pruett, M. (1995). Strategic groups and the analysis of market structure and industry dynamics. *British Journal of Management, 6,* 257–270.

Olusoga, S. A., Mokwa, M. P., & Noble, C. H. (1995). Strategic groups, mobility barriers, and competitive advantage: An empirical investigation. *Journal of Business Research, 33,* 153–164.

Owen, B. M., & Wildman, S. S. (1992). *Video economics.* Cambridge, MA: Harvard University Press.

Paul Kagan Associates, Inc. (2000). *Economics of basic cable networks 2000 databook.* New York: Author.

Porter, M. E. (1985). *Competitive advantage: Creating and sustaining superior performance.* New York: Free Press.

Punj, G., & Stewart, D. W. (1983). Cluster analysis in marketing research. *Journal of Marketing Research, 20,* 134–148.

Veliyath, R., & Ferris, S. P. (1997). Agency influences on risk reduction and operating performance: An empirical investigation among strategic groups. *Journal of Business Research, 39,* 219–230.

Waterman, D., & Weiss, A. A. (1997). *Vertical integration in cable television.* Cambridge, MA: MIT Press.

JOURNAL OF MEDIA ECONOMICS, *15*(3), 175–191

Market Structure and Local Signal Carriage Decisions in the Cable Television Industry: Results From Count Analysis

Michael Zhaoxu Yan
Department of Communication Studies
University of Michigan

Using historical data collected by the U.S. General Accounting Office (GAO) in 1990 (GAO, 1990), a time when the must-carry rules were not in effect, this study empirically tested the effects of horizontal concentration, vertical integration, and other system-specific variables on cable operators' carriage decisions regarding local television stations. Results from the negative binomial regression model (a count model) indicate that horizontal concentration or firm size had a negative effect on cable system carriage of local broadcast stations, holding other factors constant. However, the study did not find any significant vertical integration effects on such carriage.

In the United States, cable system operators are required by law to dedicate some of their cable channels to the free carriage of local broadcast stations, if the stations so demand (Cable Television Consumer Protection and Competition Act of 1992). These so-called must-carry rules have caused many controversies regarding their constitutionality and economic efficiency (see Fitzgerald, 1997; Vita, 1997).

The battle of signal carriage between the broadcasting and cable industries started as early as the 1950s when broadcasters began to push for the implementation of various forms of signal carriage rules to limit cable's impact on broadcasting. The culmination of the early regulations was the Federal Communications Commission's (FCC) 1972 *Cable Television Report and Order* (FCC, 1972). In the

---

Requests for reprints should be sent to Michael Zhaoxu Yan, Department of Communication Studies, University of Michigan, 2050B Frieze Building, 105 South State Street, Ann Arbor, MI 48109. E-mail: zyan@umich.edu

mid-1980s, the U.S. Court of Appeals for the District of Columbia struck down the must-carry rules on two occasions, ruling that although the government had a substantial interest in ensuring the continued viability of the over-the-air television system, the must-carry rules were not narrowly tailored to achieve the identified governmental interest (*Quincy Cable v. FCC*, 1985; *Century Communications Corp. v. FCC*, 1987/1988). The battle, however, raged on. In 1992, Congress passed the Cable Television Consumer Protection and Competition Act of 1992 and codified a new scheme of signal carriage regulation.[1] The 1992 must-carry rules were immediately challenged in court. After years of litigation, the U.S. Supreme Court finally upheld the constitutionality of the must-carry rules (*Turner Broadcasting System Inc. v. FCC*, 1997).[2]

Congress reestablished the must-carry rules to preserve the benefits of free, over-the-air local broadcast television and to promote the widespread dissemination of information from a multiplicity of sources (these are traditional must-carry objectives). It also wanted to promote fair competition in the television programming market. The last aim of the rules reflected the government's growing concern with the market power of the cable industry in the 1990s.

Proponents of the must-carry regulations argue that without regulations, cable systems will take advantage of whatever market power they may have to adopt adverse carriage actions against broadcasters. Specifically, broadcasters allege that vertically integrated cable systems favor networks with which they are affiliated and are thus motivated to discriminate against local broadcast stations. Similarly, they argue that larger local cable systems have the desire and market power to discontinue carriage of weaker local television stations to increase their share of the local advertising market. Although this anticompetitive theory seems to have prevailed and the must-carry rules survived the legal challenge, no factual evidence was presented or debated regarding cable systems' broadcast signal carriage behavior.[3]

---

[1] Under the 1992 must-carry rules, a television station can choose either retransmission consent or must carry. If choosing the former, a station negotiates with cable systems in its area of dominant influence (ADI) for specific carriage terms (including monetary compensation). In the latter option, cable systems within an ADI are obliged to carry the signals of local commercial television stations and qualified low-power stations without charge if the stations so request.

[2] The FCC's decision to defend the must-carry rules as non-content-based economic regulation was critical to the government's successful defense of the rules. The majority of the Supreme Court ultimately accepted the FCC's defense and upheld the must-carry rules as constitutional using an intermediate scrutiny standard (i.e., the O'Brien Test; United States v. O'Brien, 1967).

[3] In its *Turner Broadcasting System, Inc. v. FCC* (1997) decision, the Supreme Court did not judge the validity of the must-carry rules in association with the governmental goal to promote fair competition. It seemed as if the goal of the must-carry rules was solely to protect the economic viability of the broadcasting industry and whether cable operators' noncarriage action actually hurt competition simply did not matter.

Some broadcast stations were denied carriage by some cable systems in the late 1980s when must-carry rules were not in force. A 1988 survey conducted by the FCC (FCC, 1988) found that out of 4,303 responding cable systems, 869 systems (i.e., 20.2%) indicated that they dropped or denied carriage to 704 television stations in 1,820 incidents (p. 10).[4] Again, although the reasons behind these noncarriage instances have not been examined empirically, broadcasters argued that decisions to drop or deny cable carriage to local television stations were anticompetitive.

In this study, I explain cable operators' carriage or noncarriage behavior with respect to local television signal carriage by empirically testing the effects of horizontal concentration, vertical integration, and other structural factors on their carriage decisions. This is accomplished by first discussing the possible effects of structural factors such as vertical integration and horizontal concentration on local signal carriage decisions. Next, I describe the methodology and empirical models used in the study. Finally, I present and discuss the study's results.

MARKET STRUCTURE AND LOCAL SIGNAL CARRIAGE

Given the long history of must-carry regulation requiring cable systems to carry all (or most) local television signals, it is no surprise that very few studies have analyzed cable system carriage of local television stations as a dependent variable.[5] Hence, when the output level of the cable industry is examined, output behavior is usually measured as the number of cable networks offered by a cable system (e.g., Emmons & Prager, 1997). Similarly, when the effects of vertical and horizontal integration on program supply have been studied, the focus has been on the availability of cable networks (basic or pay) on local cable systems rather than on local broadcast station availability (e.g., Chipty, 1995; Ford & Jackson, 1997). Thus, the existing literature provides little information on how cable systems make their carriage decisions with respect to local broadcasting stations.

In a perfectly competitive market, a signal will be added (or dropped) if carriage of the signal will bring about benefits greater (or smaller) than the opportunity cost. A cable system's signal carriage choice is thus contingent on many factors that reflect the system's cost and demand conditions, as well as its market structure. Because of the cable industry's dominant role in local multichannel video distribution, the effects of vertical integration and horizontal concentration on pro-

---

[4]The average incidence of drop or deny that affected stations experienced was 2.59 (1,820 divided by 704). In 1992, a local broadcast station was carried by 53 cable systems on average.

[5]The only exception I know of is Crandall & Furchtgott-Roth (1996), which estimated the number of local broadcast stations carried on cable but presented the results only in an appendix with no discussion.

gram offerings by cable systems have long been a subject of policy debate (see Waterman & Weiss, 1997).

There are both efficiency-enhancing and strategic reasons for vertical integration and horizontal concentration (Waterman & Weiss, 1997). Cable firms become vertically integrated with program suppliers to enhance transaction efficiency and to strengthen the cable program supply industry by providing it with needed resources. Both motivations, however, may lead to barriers of access to subscribers for unaffiliated program suppliers, including broadcasters. For example, vertically integrated cable firms can achieve transaction efficiency by reducing or eliminating so-called double marginalization. That is, integrated cable systems pay input (programming) prices at the marginal cost level and thus perceive lower marginal cost in providing cable services. Such efficiencies are likely to result in lower final-market prices. However, this also implies that for two closely substitutive networks, one affiliated and the other not, it would be more profitable to carry the former than the latter. Thus, networks unaffiliated with cable systems may have less chance to be carried.

Vertically integrated cable operators may also strategically deny unaffiliated networks access to their subscribers. They are more likely to do so because of their financial and carriage commitment to their own cable networks. By taking advantage of the economies of scale in networking, integrated systems could potentially raise a rival network's cost and its vulnerability to competition by excluding or otherwise disadvantaging the rival network (e.g., demanding that the rival network pay the cable operator for carriage).

Empirical studies of price differentials and carriage decisions in the presence of vertical integration have shown inconsistent results (Ford & Jackson, 1997; Salinger, 1988; Waterman, 1993, 1996; Waterman & Weiss, 1996). In particular, nonintegrated cable systems do not always pay higher program prices, nor are they systematically denied access to programs affiliated with other multiple system operators (MSOs).

A related issue about the effects of industry structure on cable programming supply involves cable industry horizontal concentration. Similar to the case of vertical integration, horizontal integration has both efficiency and potentially anticompetitive effects. The industry typically argues that mergers have the potential to improve efficiency due to, for example, fixed or marginal cost savings. This implies that larger cable firms with lower marginal costs could supply more cable services at all price levels (Chipty, 1995; Otsuka, 1997).

However, larger firms could also gain more bargaining power over program suppliers, which may be used for securing lower prices or even outright carriage denial to certain networks. For example, given the competitive relation between the broadcasting and cable industries, cable systems may favor carriage of cable networks over local broadcast stations, especially if the bargaining power of the systems, conferred by their larger sizes, leads to favorable deals with cable networks. In addition, refusal to deal by larger size firms is more plausible because bigger firms could be expected to profit more from foreclosure.

As discussed previously, vertical integration and horizontal concentration may have adverse effects on cable television program supply. However, the actual effect on the carriage of a particular signal depends on other factors as well. For example, regarding the carriage of a local broadcast signal vis-à-vis a cable network in the absence of must-carry rules, a cable operator's carriage decision depends on the popularity of each broadcast station, the price of carrying each station, and the benefit to be gained by replacing a broadcast station with a cable network. Even in the absence of must-carry rules, most local television stations were carried by cable operators. This occurred because in spite of the steady decline in their viewing shares, broadcast stations still garner higher ratings than cable networks. This was especially true in the late 1980s. Likewise, cable operators normally pay license fees for the right to carry a cable network, whereas the carriage of local broadcast signals has been virtually free (Besen, Manning, & Mitchell, 1978). On the other hand, some cable operators chose to drop some local television stations and replace them with cable program networks. One reason for this behavior is the possible negative impact on an existing cable channel lineup from carrying certain local stations. Interested in maximizing the total audience of its channels as a whole, a cable system operator tends to avoid product competition from program duplication. Therefore, for example, if the broadcast station at issue were a duplicate network station or an independent station somewhat substitutive of an existing cable service, a cable system would have a disincentive to carry this station. An additional disincentive is that local stations do not offer cable systems local advertising insertions.[6] These factors may mitigate or worsen the possible negative effects of vertical and horizontal integration.

Hypotheses

Cable's signal carriage choices are determined by a range of factors that represent demand, cost, and market structure conditions in cable television. In trying to explain cable's local signal carriage behaviors, in this study I emphasized the effects of two factors: vertical integration and horizontal concentration. The main hypotheses tested in the study were

H1:   Cable systems owned by cable MSOs that have an ownership interest in a larger number of cable program networks carry fewer broadcast signals, all other things equal.

---

[6]Although a cable operator and a broadcaster could negotiate such a deal if they wanted to, I am unaware of the existence of any such deals.

H2:   Cable systems owned by larger cable MSOs carry fewer broadcast signals, all other things equal.

In addition to these two market structure variables, I included other system-specific variables such as system penetration rates, channel capacity, plant miles, system age, television market size, and the availability of local market stations. However, station-specific variables such as station type, popularity, and distance from the cable headend are not included in the analysis here.[7]

METHOD

Data and Variables

The main data source for this study is the U.S. General Accounting Office (GAO; 1990) *Follow-Up National Survey of Cable Television Rates and Services.* In addition to detailed data on cable rates and service offerings, the GAO survey gathered information on the availability of local broadcast stations on sampled cable systems in 1984, 1986, and 1989. The survey was sent to 1,971 cable systems that were selected using a random and stratified sampling method. The response rate was approximately 78% (1,529 cable systems).[8] The electronic version of the database obtained for this study removed all system identifications (such as system name and address) except their central zip codes to ensure confidentiality. Using the *National 5-Digit ZIP Code and Post Office Directory* (1991), I was able to identify 1,413 cable systems out of the 1,417 observations that had zip code information. Excluding those systems located in Puerto Rico, Hawaii, the Virgin Islands, and Alaska, the final sample for this study includes 1,359 observations.[9] Additional system and demographic data were collected from the *Television and Cable Factbook* (1990), *Broadcasting Yearbook* (1990), *City and County Data Book* (1994), and *Investing in Television* (1990). Table 1 lists the dependent and independent variables used in the regression models, their data sources, and selected summary statistics.

The dependent variable is the number of local broadcast stations that would have been qualified for carriage under must carry but were not carried by a cable

---

[7]The omission of station-specific variables is due to data constraints. The data set used in this study is secondary and contains no station-specific information. Manually collecting station information for each cable system in the sample seems infeasible, if possible at all.

[8]See GAO (1990) for sampling methodology, summary statistics, and the questionnaire. The GAO reported that there were 1,530 observations, but the electronic database I obtained contained only 1,529.

[9]The main reason for excluding systems from these regions is that Arbitron does not have ADI markets for these areas.

TABLE 1
Variable List and Summary Statistics

Variable	M	SD	No. Observations	Description	Source
LNSUB	12.46	2.626	1,358	(log) No. of cable subscribers nationwide a system owner owns	2
MSO	0.965	0.183	1,359	If a system owner is an MSO (1 = yes)	2
TOP25	0.578	0.494	1,322	If a system owner is a Top 25 MSO (1 = yes)	1
VI_TOT	4.809	7.703	1,359	No. of cable networks with which a system owner is vertically integrated	2, 4, 5
VI_N	3.849	6.05	1,359	No. of national cable networks with which a system owner is vertically integrated	2, 4, 5
VI	0.414	0.493	1,359	If a system owner is vertically integrated (1 = yes)	2, 4, 5
SYSPENE (89)	0.549	0.359	1,257	Penetration rate of a cable system in its franchise area (1989)	1
SYSPENE (88)	0.544	0.356	1,127	Penetration rate of a cable system in its franchise area (1988)	1
SYSSHARE (88)	0.037	0.082	1,354	Subscriber share of a cable system in its ADI (1988)	1, 3
CAP	39.331	15.259	1,341	Channel capacity of a cable system	1
MILE	317.221	579.588	1,335	Plant miles of a cable system	1
AGE	11.164	8.021	1,335	Age of cable system as of 1989	1
LOCAL (89)	7.048	3.395	1,342	No. of local stations carried by a system (1989)	3
LOCAL (84)	6.795	3.567	1,274	No. of local stations carried by a system (1984)	3
OTA_A	10.74	5.491	1,359	No. of stations available in a system's ADI	3
VIEW_CABLE	24.971	12.001	1,359	All day household viewing share of cable networks in a system ADI	6
RANK_A	66.48	52.45	1,359	Rank of a system's ADI	3
RETAO:	5619.38	1956.83	1,359	Per capital retail sales in a system's county (1987)	7
NDROP	0.399	1.035	1,274	No. of stations not carried by a cable system	1

Note. The data are for the end of 1989, unless otherwise indicated. MSO = multiple system operator; ADI = area of dominant influence. Data sources are

1. General Accounting Office (1990).
2. *Television and Cable Factbook* (1990).
3. *Cable and Station Coverage Atlas* (1990).
4. Paul Kagan Associates, Inc (1989, p. 3).
5. FCC (1990, Appendix G, Table VI).
6. *Investing in Television* (1990).
7. *City and County Data Book* (1994).

181

system on December 31, 1989 (*NDROP*). *NDROP* is constructed in two steps. First, the number of stations dropped or denied carriage due to the lifting of must-carry rules for each station type (*M*), $NDROP_i$ (i = 1 for network affiliate station, 2 for commercial independent station, or 3 for public and other type stations), was computed by subtracting the total number of a particular type of local stations a system carried in 1989 from the number in 1984.[10] A negative $NDROP_i$ value indicates no dropping and was set to zero. In the second step, *NDROP* was computed by adding up the $NDROP_i$ values. That is

$$NDROP = \sum_{i=1}^{M} \left(NDROP_{i,1984} - NDROP_{i,1989} \right),$$

where $NDROP_{i,1984} - NDROP_{i,1989} = 0$, if < 0; $M = 3$. The resulting *NDROP* has a mean value of 0.399 and the vast majority of the systems (over 79.1%) did not drop any station.[11] The noncarriage rate of about 20% in the sample is comparable to the result from the 1988 FCC broadcast signal carriage survey (FCC, 1988).

The independent variables of main interest in this study pertain to horizontal concentration and vertical integration.[12] Several measures for each category are included. The main size variable, *LNSUB,* is the total number of subscribers owned by a system's MSO.[13] A second size variable is a dummy variable (*TOP25*) indicating if a cable system was owned by a Top 25 MSO. Finally, *SYSSHARE,* the percentage of cable subscribers within a cable system's ADI that were owned by a cable system, is included to test if larger cable systems relative to the size of their ADI dropped more television stations.

The main vertical integration measure is *VI_N,* the number of national cable networks with which a cable system's owner is affiliated. An alternative measure of vertical integration is *VI_TOT,* which includes both national and regional cable

---

[10]For cable systems built after 1984, the 1986 number is used. Station carriage data for systems built after 1986 were not available. This accounts for most of the missing data for *NDROP.*

[11]This way of constructing *NDROP* has its problems, caused by the nature of the data that makes it impossible to examine each station individually for carriage status. First, the number of stations continued to grow during 1985 to 1989; therefore, *NDROP* would not be accurately measured (i.e., underestimated) in cable markets that had new station(s). Second, for those markets that experienced no station growth during this period, it is still possible, although unlikely, that a cable system might drop a qualified station and add an unqualified station and maintain the same number of local stations on its system in 1984 and 1989. In this study, I assumed that, to the extent the aforementioned scenarios were true, they were across all system levels (i.e., they occurred in a random fashion).

[12]All data for the independent variables are for the end of 1989 unless otherwise specified.

[13]Many MSOs have common ownership. For example, at the time of this study, TCI owned 50% of Bresnan, 100% of Heritage, and 54% of United Artists, among others. *LNSUB* does not take this into account.

networks.[14] As stated in the hypotheses, I expected *NDROP* to be positively correlated with the size and vertical integration variables.

On average, vertically integrated MSOs tend to be larger than nonvertically integrated cable operators.[15] As discussed earlier, larger firm size can reinforce both efficiency and anticompetitive effects of vertical integration. Thus, bigger and vertically integrated cable systems may carry even fewer stations. To test this hypothesis, an interaction term, *HI*VI*, which equals *LNSUB* times *VI_N*, is included in one of the variations of the empirical models.

The remaining independent variables in Table 1 are included to control for different demand, cost, and competitive situations across cable systems. The effect of *SYSPENE*, the penetration rate of a cable system in its franchise area, on cable local carriage is not clear. High penetration systems often exist in smaller markets with fewer over-the-air television stations or in markets in which there are significant reception problems with respect to local broadcast stations. In these markets, the demand for cable television is relatively inelastic, suggesting that cable systems in these markets could drop or carry fewer local stations without incurring much subscription loss. High penetration systems may also choose to carry more cable networks over broadcast stations to maintain their penetration rate if high penetration rate reflects customers' preference for cable networks over local broadcast stations. However, cable systems in low penetration rate areas (such as big television markets) may also want to carry more cable networks to entice households to subscribe to cable television.[16]

One of the reasons consumers subscribe to cable is to improve reception quality of over-the-air broadcast signals. Thus, one would always expect cable systems to carry some local broadcast stations. However, the more local stations a cable system carries, the less marginal benefit the carriage of an additional station would generate and the more likely the system will stop carrying one or more local stations in the absence of must-carry rules. The number of broadcast stations already carried on a cable system in 1984 is included to test this effect (*LOCAL84*).[17]

---

[14]A cable system operator or owner was considered to be vertically integrated with a cable network if it had a 5% or greater interest in the cable network. For those interested in obtaining an appendix explaining how the vertical integration variable was constructed, please contact Michael Zhaoxu Yan.

[15]In this sample, *LNSUB* and *VI* are moderately correlated, $r = .654, p < .0001$.

[16]The variable *SYSPENE* is endogenous; that is, local signal carriage and penetration rate influence each other. To avoid this problem, in this study I used the 1988 system penetration data. The penetration data in the sample for the 2 years (1988 and 1989) are highly correlated, $r = .993, p < .0001$ ($N = 1,171$).

[17]The 1984 (rather than 1989) number is used to avoid endogeneity problems. Using the 1984 data has another advantage. Assuming that all of the local stations were carried by cable systems in 1984, due to the mandate of the must-carry rules, the variable *LOCAL84* also represents the availability of broadcast stations in each system's local market in 1984. Similarly, the more stations that are available in a market, the more likely one or more of the stations will not be carried.

One important factor influencing a cable operator's local carriage decisions is how many people like to watch broadcast stations compared to cable networks. If cable network programs were relatively more popular than broadcast fare in one ADI versus another, cable systems would be more likely to carry fewer broadcast stations and reserve the channel space for cable networks as a result of increased subscriber demand for cable network programming. On the other hand, if the reverse were true, cable operators might still choose to carry fewer broadcast stations relative to cable networks to try and increase consumer demand for cable network programming. The variable *VIEW_CABLE*, measuring the viewing share of cable program networks in a system's ADI in July 1989, was used to determine which of these theories is correct. *NDROP* and *VIEW_CABLE* were expected to have a positive relation if the former situation occurs and a negative relation if the latter theory holds true.

CAP, MILE, and *AGE* are cost variables. Greater channel capacity and more plant miles mean lower marginal cost with respect to signal carriage and other system operations. This should lead to the carriage of more total channels, local or cable. The effect of *AGE*, however, is ambiguous. Older systems may be more efficient and carry more local channels, but they may also have smaller channel capacity if they have not been renovated, leading to station dropping.

RETAIL is the amount of retail sales per capita in a system's county in 1987. If the theory is true that cable systems deny carrying broadcast stations to reap local advertising revenues, then one would expect that this happens more often in relatively rich areas. *RETAIL* is included to test this assumption.

Finally, *RANK_A,* the rank of the ADI in which a cable system is located, is included to indicate the competitiveness between the cable television and broadcasting industries in each television market. It is assumed that the lower the ADI rank number, the more competitive the television market. The effect of *RANK_A* on station carriage can be both positive and negative. Because the probability of a station not being carried on cable systems in bigger markets (with lower rank numbers) is actually higher than in smaller markets, the coefficient estimate of *RANK_A* can be negative. However, because households in bigger markets generally have higher reservation utilities with respect to cable subscription due to the availability of more local broadcast stations, a positive effect would result if cable systems in more competitive markets carry more local stations to try to lure television households to subscribe to cable television.

Empirical Models

The dependent variable in this study, $NDROP_i$, includes only nonnegative (including zero) and discrete integral values. Therefore, the usual normal assumption for regression analysis does not apply here. Instead, I used count models to account for the special nature of the dependent variable. Initially, four count models were specified—the Poisson regression model, the negative binomial regression model, the zero-inflated Poisson model, and the zero-inflated negative binomial model. After a series of empirical tests were performed to identify the best estimating model, the negative binomial regression model emerged as the most robust functional form. Therefore, the results provided in this study are based exclusively on the negative binomial regression model estimates.[18]

RESULTS

The size variable *LNSUB* had a positive effect on *NDROP* (β = .143, p < .01; see Table 2, Model V). That is, larger cable firms dropped more local broadcast stations. Specifically, a 1% increase in the number of a cable MSO's subscribers increased noncarriage occurrences by a factor of .154, holding all other variables constant.[19]

I also tested the hypothesis that the largest MSOs may drop even more stations than other cable system owners (*LNSUB*TOP25*). However, this hypothesis was not supported. Likewise, no significant effect was found for the vertical integration variable *VI_N*. In addition, the results show no support for the assumption that larger MSOs with financial interests in more cable program networks carry fewer stations (*LNSUB*VI_N* and *TOP25*VI_N*).

A cable system's share of subscribers in its own ADI (*SYSSHARE*) also did not affect the system's carriage behavior. This suggests that with respect to local signal carriage, an individual cable system's size, relative to the size of its local media market, does not have a significant effect. On the other hand, a system's penetration rate in its franchise area (*SYSPENE*) was found to have a significantly positive effect on *NDROP* (β = .409, p = .08). Specifically, a 1% increase in a system's penetration rate increased noncarriage instances by a factor of .505, holding all other variables constant.

The effect of cable viewing (*VIEW_CABLE*) turned out to be negative, indicating that more local station viewing by cable subscribers relative to cable network viewing in a system's ADI increased noncarriage of broadcast stations. A 1% increase in local viewing shares increased noncarriage instances by a factor of .024. This result is consistent with the theory that cable systems carry fewer broadcast stations for anticompetitive reasons.

---

[18]For those interested in obtaining a technical appendix providing a detailed discussion of the four count models used in this study, the empirical estimates generated from estimating each of the alternative count models, and the reasons behind the selection of the negative binomial regression model as the best estimating model for this study, please contact Michael Zhaoxu Yan. See Cameron & Trivedi (1998) for a detailed discussion on estimating count models.

[19]The marginal effects reported are factor changes in *NDROP* due to a one-unit change in each independent variable (k). Marginal effects were calculated using the following formula:

$$\frac{E\left(y|x, x_k + 1\right)}{E\left(y|x, x_k\right)} = e^{\beta_k}.$$

TABLE 2
Results of Negative Binomial Regression Models

Dependent Variable NDROP	Models				
	I	II	III	IV	V
INTERCEPT	-3.668***	-3.555***	-3.325***	-4.010***	-4.040***
	(-5.779)	(-5.546)	(-4.352)	(-4.542)	(-4.392)
LNSUB	0.078**	0.067*	0.078**	0.141***	0.143***
	(2.048)	(1.743)	(2.042)	(2.625)	(2.540)
TOP25				1.698	1.352
				(1.222)	(0.804)
LNSUB × TOP25				-0.146	-0.121
				(-1.365)	(-0.935)
VL_N	-0.023		-0.023	-0.011	0.057
	(-1.459)		(-1.456)	(-0.621)	(0.277)
VL_TOT		-0.013			
		(-1.070)			
LNSUB × VL_N					-0.005
					(-0.367)
TOP25 × VL_N					-0.001
					(-0.013)
SYSSHARE (88)			0.496	0.603	0.544
			(0.428)	(0.494)	(0.436)
SYSPENE(88)	0.363	0.369	0.398*	0.406*	0.409*
	(1.603)	(1.632)	(1.718)	(1.753)	(1.755)
VIEW_CABLE	-0.029***	-0.029***	-0.025***	-0.024***	-0.024***
	(-3.404)	(-3.405)	(-2.465)	(-2.395)	(-2.411)
LOCAL (84)	0.303***	0.304***	0.303***	0.298***	0.298***
	(13.357)	(13.424)	(13.286)	(12.976)	(12.929)
CAP	-0.029***	-0.029***	-0.029***	-0.028***	-0.028***
	(-7.151)	(-7.214)	(-7.272)	(-6.866)	(-6.737)

MILE	0.000	0.000	0.000	0.000	0.000
	(0.494)	(0.517)	(0.180)	(0.143)	(0.149)
AGE	-0.025	-0.024	-0.023	-0.027	-0.027
	(-0.827)	(-0.796)	(-0.741)	(-0.876)	(-0.880)
AGE × AGE	0.001	0.001	0.001	0.001	0.001
	(0.976)	(0.965)	(0.905)	(1.052)	(1.055)
RETAIL	0.000	0.000	0.000	0.000	0.000
	(1.195)	(1.171)	(1.256)	(1.248)	(1.200)
RANK_A	0.009***	0.009***	0.008***	0.008***	0.008***
	(4.378)	(4.335)	(3.795)	(3.413)	(3.354)
N	1,058	1,058	1,056	1,033	1,033

Note. Regression coefficients with *t* ratios are in parentheses. NDROP = no. of stations not carried by a cable system on December 31, 1989; LNSUB = no. of cable subscribers nationwide a system owner owns; TOP25 = If a system owner is a Top 25 multiple system operator; VI = vertically integrated; VI_N = no. of national cable networks with which a system owner is VI; VI_TOT = includes both national and regional cable networks; ADI = area of dominant influence; SYSSHARE (88) = subscriber share of a cable system in its ADI (1988); SYSPENE (88) = penetration rate of a cable system in its franchise area (1988); VIEW_CABLE = all day household viewing share of cable networks in a system's ADI; LOCAL (84) = no. of local stations carried by a system (1984); CAP = channel capacity of a cable system; MILE = plant miles of a cable system; AGE = age of a cable system as of 1989; RETAIL = amount of retail sales per capita in a system's county in 1987; RANK_A = rank of the ADI in which a cable system is located.

*p < .10. **p < .05. ***p < .01.

As expected, *LOCAL(84)*, the carriage of more broadcast stations on a local cable system, increased noncarriage instances ($\beta = .298, p < .01$). This is due to the decreasing marginal benefit of carrying additional broadcast signals. Holding all other variables constant, the carriage of an additional broadcast station on a cable system increased noncarriage by a factor of .347.

The negative effect of channel capacity (*CAP*) supports the assumption that greater channel capacity decreases the marginal cost of adding an additional channel and hence increases the chance of a local broadcast station being carried by a cable system. An extra channel of cable system capacity decreased the mean number of dropped stations by .028. However, the other cost variables, system plant miles (*MILE*) and system age (*AGE* and *AGE*AGE*), had no significant effect on cable system carriage behavior.

Retail sales in a cable system's local area (*RETAIL*) also had no significant effect on *NDROP*. However, a system's ADI rank (*RANK_A*), a variable representing the degree of competition in a local television market, has a positive effect ($\beta = .008, p < .01$). This means that cable operators in bigger markets actually dropped fewer stations, despite the fact that there are more broadcast stations available in these markets. This supports the theory that, in facing greater competition from broadcast stations in bigger markets, cable systems try to carry more broadcast stations to increase their competitive strength vis-à-vis broadcast stations and other multichannel video providers (Dertouzos & Wildman, 1998).

Finally, a number of variations to the Model V regression results are provided in Table 2. The coefficient estimates of these alternative negative binomial regression models are very consistent with the Model V results.

CONCLUSION

This study systematically tested the effects of vertical integration, horizontal concentration, and other system-specific variables on cable systems' signal carriage decisions regarding local broadcast stations during a period when the must-carry rules were not in effect. The results support the hypothesis that horizontal concentration or larger firm size in the cable television industry has a negative effect on the carriage of local broadcast stations on cable systems, holding all other factors constant. Larger cable MSOs have shown lower marginal costs with respect to program supply and, as a result, tend to supply more cable channels (Chipty, 1995). The results provided here are consistent with the theory that larger MSOs dropped a larger number of over-the-air television stations to add more cable networks to their lineups.

The results also confirm that the cable and broadcasting industries compete with each other. Cable operators in bigger markets with greater competition from other video delivery systems (including broadcasting) carried more local broadcast stations to increase their relative competitiveness. In addition, more local station viewing by cable subscribers relative to cable network viewing increased noncarriage instances. The latter finding implies that cable's noncarriage behavior has anticompetitive motivations.

Likewise, I found that more noncarriage occurred in higher penetration cable systems and in smaller ADIs in which cable subscribers register more local station viewing. This suggests that noncarriage may be more serious in small or rural areas, and it raises a public policy issue about the long-term viability of local broadcast stations in already fragile small markets without the umbrella protection of the must-carry rules.

Additionally, the results indicate that although an increase in the number of local broadcast stations carried by a cable system (and by implication, an increase in the number of local market stations) increases the likelihood of broadcast station noncarriage by cable operators, the expansion of cable system capacity eases the pressure on cable systems and makes the carriage of additional stations possible.

Finally, contrary to the original hypothesis, no significant effect with respect to vertical integration was found in this study. This may be due to measurement problems. Counting the number of cable networks a cable MSO owns is a crude way of measuring cable firms' programming interests. For example, a firm with 100% ownership of one single network may have more control over program decisions than another firm that has a 10% interest in each of 10 cable networks.

Taken together, the results raise issues regarding the motivations behind cable's noncarriage behavior. They lend some support to the necessity of the must-carry rules, at least in smaller markets. On the other hand, the findings suggest that as cable systems continue to expand their channel capacity and as the video distribution market becomes more competitive, the need for government-mandated must-carry rules may not be as great as before.

Very few studies have analyzed the must-carry rules from an economic perspective. In this study I partially fill this gap in the current literature by providing a systematic analysis of the cable industry's broadcast signal carriage behavior. This was made possible because of the unique window opened by the repeal of the must-carry rules in the late 1980s and the availability of the historical GAO data. However, the reliance on secondary data also imposes limitations on this study.

Specifically, the station-specific variables, although certainly affecting cable operators' decisions with respect to local station carriage, are not included in the models estimated in this study. Any inference about the nature of cable system noncarriage instances (that is, whether they are anticompetitively motivated) necessitates the examination of the actual stations being denied carriage. To the extent that these variables are not controlled for, the results here say little about whether the noncarriage instances are efficient or anticompetitive and whether the must-carry regulations are justifiable from an economic policy perspective.

ACKNOWLEDGMENT

I thank David Waterman of Indiana University and Mike Wirth of the University of Denver for their helpful comments on the original manuscript. George S. Ford of Z-Tel Communications provided the data used in the study. His generosity is gratefully acknowledged. Last, but not least, I thank the Magness Institute for its financial support for conducting this study.

REFERENCES

Besen, S., Manning, W., Jr., & Mitchell, B. (1978). Copyright liability for cable television: Compulsory licensing and the Coase theorem. *Journal of Law and Economics, 212,* 67–95.
Broadcasting yearbook. (1990). Washington, DC: Broadcasting Publications Inc.
Cable and station coverage atlas. (1990). Washington, DC: Warren Publishing.
Cable Television Consumer Protection and Competition Act of 1992, Pub. L. No. 102–385, § 4 and 5, 106 Stat. 1460 (1992).
Cameron, A. C., & Trivedi, P. K. (1998). *Regression analysis of count data.* Cambridge, England: Cambridge University Press.
Century Communications Corp. v. FCC, 835 F.2d 292 (D.C. Cir. 1987), *cert. denied,* 108 S. Ct. 2018 (1988).
Chipty, T. (1995). Horizontal integration for bargaining power: Evidence from the cable television industry. *Journal of Economics and Management Strategy, 4,* 375–397.
City and county data book. (1994). Washington, DC: U.S. Census Bureau.
Crandall, R., & Furchtgott-Roth, H. (1996). *Cable TV: Regulation or competition?* Washington, DC: Brookings Institute.
Dertouzos, J., & Wildman, S. (1998). Regulatory standards: The effects of broadcast signals on cable television. In R. Noll & M. Price (Eds.), *A communications cornucopia: Markle Foundation essays on information policy.* Washington, DC: Brookings Institution Press.
Emmons, W., & Prager, R. (1997). The effects of market structure and ownership on prices and service offerings in the U.S. cable television industry. R*AND Journal of Economics, 28,* 732–750.
Federal Communications Commission. (1972). *Cable television report and order,* 36 FCC 2d 143.
Federal Communications Commission. (1988, September 1). *Cable System Broadcast Signal Carriage Survey Report.* Washington, DC: Author.
Federal Communications Commission. (1990). *In the matter of competition, rate deregulation and the Commission's policies relating to the provision of cable television service; Report,* 67 Rad. Reg. 2d (P&F) 1771.
Fitzgerald, M. D. (1997). Constitutional law—Congressional regulation of cable television—Upholding the must-carry provisions of the Cable Television Consumer Protection and Competition Act of 1992. *Tennessee Law Review, 65,* 319.
Ford, G., & Jackson, J. (1997). Horizontal concentration and vertical integration in the cable television industry. *Review of Industrial Organization, 12,* 501–518.
General Accounting Office. (1990, June 13). *Follow-up national survey of cable television rates and services.* Washington, DC: Author.
Investing in television. (1990). Washington, DC: BIA Publications.
National 5-digit ZIP Code and post office directory. (1991). Washington, DC: U.S. Postal Service.
Otsuka, Y. (1997). A welfare analysis of local franchise and other types of regulation: Evidence from the cable TV industry. *Journal of Regulatory Economics, 11,* 157–180.

Paul Kagan Associates, Inc. (1989, December 20). *Cable TV programming* (p. 3). Carmel, CA: Author.

Quincy Cable v. FCC, 768 F.2d 1434 (D.C. Cir. 1985).

Salinger, M. (1988). *A test of successive monopoly and foreclosure effects: Vertical integration between cable systems and pay services.* Unpublished manuscript, Graduate School of Business, Columbia University, New York.

Television and cable factbook. (1990). Washington, DC: Warren Publishing.

Turner Broadcasting System Inc. v. FCC, 520 U.S. 180 (1997).

Vita, M. (1993). Must-carry regulations for cable television systems: An economic policy analysis. *Journal of Broadcasting and Economic Media, 37,* 1–19.

United States v. O'Brien, 391 U.S. 367 (1967).

Waterman, D. (1993). A model of vertical integration and economics of scale in information product distribution. *Journal of Media Economics, 6*(3), 23–35.

Waterman, D. (1996). Local monopsony and free riders. *Information Economics and Policy, 8,* 337–355.

Waterman, D., & Weiss, A. (1996). The effects of vertical integration between cable television systems and pay cable networks. *Journal of Econometrics, 72,* 357–395.

Waterman, D., & Weiss, A. (1997). *Vertical integration in cable television.* Cambridge, MA: MIT Press.

JOURNAL OF MEDIA ECONOMICS, *15*(3), 193–207

Digital Cable: Exploring Factors Associated With Early Adoption

Myung-Hyun Kang
School of Communication
Hallym University, Korea

Digital cable is a technological innovation featuring interactivity, which is still in its infancy. This study identifies a profile of early digital cable subscribers based on a telephone survey. The study results indicate that digital cable subscribers are more likely to watch television, subscribe to premium services, perceive their cable operator to be technologically progressive, and express greater satisfaction with current cable service compared to analog-only subscribers. It was also found that the more people watch television, have premium channels, and evaluate their cable operator as innovative toward technology, the sooner they can be expected to upgrade to new cable services. Implications for cable service structuring and marketing behaviors are also discussed.

Since the late 1990s, cable companies have offered an upgraded distribution system: digital cable. For about $10 a month over the cost of an analog cable package, a subscriber can upgrade to digital cable featuring interactivity. The purpose of this study was to understand and predict digital cable adoption by identifying a profile of early digital subscribers along with implications for digital cable service structuring and approaches to marketing.

The research questions (RQs) on which this article focuses are as follows:

RQ1: What factors are most important in determining whether consumers choose to be early adopters of digital cable?

RQ2: What factors are most important in determining consumer adoptive innovativeness (i.e., the speed of consumer adoption) with respect to digital cable?

Requests for reprints should be sent to Myung-Hyun Kang, School of Communication, Hallym University, Okchon-dong, Chunchon, Kangwon-do, Korea 200–702. E-mail: mhkang@hallym.ac.kr

In this study, I attempt to answer these questions by discussing digital cable's potential for generating new products for consumers and additional revenue streams for cable entrepreneurs, discussing diffusion theory and using it to provide a theoretical frame for the analysis, providing a set of hypotheses that were empirically tested, describing the methods used to conduct the analysis, and reporting and discussing the results obtained.

DIGITAL CABLE AS A NEW REVENUE SOURCE

Digital compression technology expands the channel capacity of analog cable. This increased capacity allows cable operators to offer current and potential subscribers a digital service tier with enhanced attributes and additional program networks not currently available on the existing analog basic service tier (Higgins, 1997). Digital cable service also typically provides a number of multiplexed premium movie channels (e.g., HBO1, HBO2, HBO3, etc.) that provide premium channel subscribers with a significant increase in pay channel program choice and variety (Colman, 1998). By offering digital subscribers multiple channels of HBO (or Showtime, Starz, or a combination, etc.), premium channel subscriber satisfaction should be increased and subscriber churn decreased (Haring, 1997). Additionally, digital cable offers more pay-per-view titles and more frequent start times than ever before. With more frequent start times, digital cable has increased viewer convenience. Because recently released hit movies are typically available at 15- to 30-min intervals, this service is referred to as *near video on demand* (NVOD; Baldwin, McVoy, & Steinfield, 1996). Finally, and perhaps most important, digital cable offers subscribers an interactive program guide, which could revolutionize the way people watch TV. The interactive guide allows users to sort through on-screen TV listings by time, channel, or themes. In a digital world with 200-plus channels, cable subscribers have to navigate through a much larger number of channels than in the analog world. Digital cable also can offer an array of new products to its consumers. Features such as two-way services or higher picture quality (i.e., high-definition television [HDTV]) may lead consumers to perceive digital cable as a new technology, separate from current analog cable service.

Because of its innovative features, the penetration rate of digital cable in the United States has been increasing since the first launch in late 1996. Media analysts estimate that as of the end of 1999, there were roughly 5.1 million digital cable subscribers, and industry predictions go as high as 42 million by the end of 2006 (Paul Kagan Associates, Inc., 1999). AT&T Broadband & Internet Services (formerly TCI) started the country's first full-fledged digital cable offering in October 1996 and had more than 1.8 million digital cable subscribers nationwide by 1999 (Higgins, 2000). The company estimated that roughly 70% of its existing analog subscribers would buy digital cable within the next 3 to 5 years. Other cable operators such as AOL Time Warner, Cox, and Comcast are in various stages of digital deployment. For example, AOL Time Warner signed up more than 0.6 million subscribers by year-end 1999 (its first year of offering digital cable service), which was beyond its original expectation (McAdams, 1999).

Most cable operators are optimistic about the new service, believing that digital cable will become their most important revenue source in the near future. Basic cable subscriber growth has been less than 2% over the past few years, and competitive pressure primarily from Direct-Broadcast Satellite (DBS) entrepreneurs continues to increase.

Digital cable is recognized as an effective means for cable companies to generate increased revenue and to keep premium customers from migrating to DBS. Digital cable has increased cash flow for several cable operators (Higgins, 2000). Some analysts in the cable industry have predicted that digital cable might be profitable with about 20% penetration in each system (Colman, 1998).

Digital cable service is still in its infancy. The obvious importance of the service to the cable industry warrants additional research. In particular, an understanding of subscribers and nonsubscribers in the initial stages of adoption could expedite diffusion of the new service. In this study, I explore the factors associated with early adoption of digital cable in an effort to predict digital cable adoption likelihood among existing analog consumers.

It is important to note that, at some point, an economic threshold will be reached in which it is practical to convert all cable subscribers to digital not necessarily too far into the adoption curve. Analog converters are aging, digital boxes will decline in cost, revenues from multiplexed pay channels will stabilize or increase, and digital channels will grow in attractiveness. This will permit a restructuring of services and multiply the number of channels recovered from the old analog service by a factor of 10. In these circumstances, NVOD, with frequent start times over many titles, subscription video on demand (SVOD), and video on demand (VOD) become feasible. Digital delivery of HDTV also becomes much more practical.

DIFFUSION THEORY

This study is based on the assumption that digital cable is an innovative technology in the area of cable telecommunications and uses diffusion theory as its theoretical framework. Diffusion theory provides a systematic demand side explanation of how new innovative technologies are communicated, evaluated, adopted, and reevaluated by consumers (Williams, Strover, & Grant, 1994). According to diffusion theory (Rogers, 1995), people's adoption behavior is a function of their socioeconomic status, media use patterns, and uses of other technologies. Furthermore, there has been another movement in diffusion research toward an innovation-centered perspective that indicates consumer attitudes toward an innovation (e.g., relative advantage, complexity, etc.) are critical to the likelihood of its diffusion. For example, Ostlund (1974) argued that the greater the perceived advantages of using an innovation, the greater the probability that it will be adopted.

Another important concept is *innovativeness*, which Rogers (1995) conceptually defined as "the degree to which an individual or other unit of adoption is *relatively earlier* [italics added] in adopting new ideas than other members of a system" (p. 22). Put another way, an individual's adoptive innovativeness reflects the relative earliness or lateness with which an innovation is adopted when compared with other members of a market. Rogers used adoptive innovativeness to classify adopters into five categories: innovators (2.5%), early adopters (13.5%), early majority (34%), late majority (34%), and laggards (16%). According to Rogers, the characteristics of earlier adopters may be different from later adopters or nonadopters due to the degree of their adoptive innovativeness.

HYPOTHESES

A great deal of diffusion research has focused on identifying demographic variables associated with earlier adopters of an innovation (Robertson, 1967; Rogers, 1995). On the basis of the diffusion literature, Rogers postulated that earlier adopters of new communication technology will be younger, better educated, and of higher income than later adopters or nonadopters. This proposition has been supported by a wide range of diffusion research about VCRs (Reagan, 1987), personal computers (Danko & MacLachlan, 1983; Dickerson & Gentry, 1983), videotex (Ettema, 1984, 1989), DBS (Bruce, 1996), HDTV (Dupagne, 1999), and the Internet (Atkin, Jeffres, & Neuendorf, 1998).

The demographic profiles associated with earlier adopters of cable subscription, including a tendency for there to be more children in a cable household (e.g., Collins, Reagan, & Abel, 1983), have been generally confirmed by past studies despite some contrary findings (see Atkin & LaRose, 1994a). Therefore, in this study I tested the following hypothesis (H) regarding demographics:

H1: Digital cable subscribers will be younger, of higher income, better educated, and have more children than nonsubscribers (i.e., analog-only subscribers) during the technology's early stages of deployment.

Diffusion theory holds that earlier adopters will use a greater variety of mass media and make heavier use of these media than later adopters (Rogers, 1995).

Media usage variables have been included in several studies to predict cable subscribership. In general, the variables include media use behaviors such as television viewing (Greenberg, Heeter, D'Alessio, & Sipes 1988; LaRose & Atkin, 1988b), radio listening (Reagan, Ducey, & Bernstein, 1985), newspaper reading (LaRose & Atkin, 1988b), and moviegoing (Collins et al., 1983; Reagan et al., 1985). Therefore, the following was hypothesized:

H2: Media use levels (i.e., TV viewing, radio listening, newspaper reading, and moviegoing) of digital cable subscribers will be higher than nonsubscribers during the technology's early stages of deployment.

Some research points to the existence of technology clusters, suggesting that the adoption of one medium is likely to stimulate the use of functionally similar media (Atkin & LaRose, 1994b; LaRose & Atkin, 1992). Ettema (1984, 1989), for instance, found that new technologies are most likely to be used if they are functionally similar to existing ones. These findings imply that individuals who have already used some premium channels and pay-per-view movies are more likely to subscribe to digital cable because they are relatively heavy users of other types of cable service. Many cable operators initially marketed their digital service primarily to premium subscribers (see Katz & Peers, 1998).

Also, subscribers taking a higher level of cable service are more likely to have used other technical products. Albarran and Umphrey (1994) found that the ownership of other related technologies such as the VCR was a predictor of cable and pay cable subscribership. Thus, the following hypotheses were posed:

H3: Premium channel subscribers will be more likely to subscribe to digital cable than nonpremium subscribers during the technology's early stages of deployment.
H4: Digital cable subscribers will have more home technical devices than nonsubscribers during the technology's early stages of deployment.

According to diffusion theory (Rogers, 1995), technological innovation adoption is related to one's innovative traits to try new products, a proposition supported by a series of studies. For example, Lin (1998) reported that computer adopter groups expressed the highest degree of need for innovativeness (e.g., willingness to learn new ideas, willingness to explore new technology, keeping up with new technology) compared with likely adopters or nonadopters. Similarly, consumers' perceived image of their cable operator as an innovator may be related to the adoption of new cable products. Results of a recent consumer survey (Petrozzello, 1997) showed that early demand for cable innovation such as the cable modem could be influenced by a cable company's high-tech image. Therefore, the following relations were hypothesized:

H5: Digital cable subscribers will perceive themselves to be more innovative than will nonsubscribers during the technology's early stages of deployment.

H6: Digital cable subscribers will perceive their cable company to be more innovative than will nonsubscribers during the technology's early stages of deployment.

Consumer satisfaction with the current cable service could also be a predictor with respect to service upgrading behavior. Earlier studies (Jacobs, 1995, 1996; LaRose & Atkin, 1988a) have suggested that once an individual subscribes to a cable service, his or her level of satisfaction with the current service might be more important to maintaining the subscription or to upgrading–downgrading behaviors than are such factors as demographics or media use behaviors. Similarly, in a study examining the determinants of cable consumer satisfaction, Jacobs (1996) observed that overall satisfaction with cable service was inversely related to subscriber complaining behavior. As Jacobs (1995) noted, the satisfaction of subscribers is certainly "more directly linked with disconnect or subscription upgrading/downgrading behaviors" (p. 271).

The last hypothesis deals with the relation between a consumer's overall satisfaction with current cable service and whether they have upgraded to digital cable:

H7: Digital cable subscribers will express higher satisfaction with their current cable service than nonsubscribers during the technology's early stages of deployment.

METHOD

To collect data for this study, a telephone survey was conducted in a single Michigan cable market where digital cable service has been available since early 1998. Two lists, one for digital subscribers and one for nondigital subscribers (analog only), were obtained from the local cable company. The lists included about 800 computer-generated random phone numbers—400 each of digital and analog—and information about whether the household subscribed to digital cable.

Interviews were conducted during the evening hours (6:00 p.m. to 9:00 p.m.) from June 8 to June 17, 1999, by paid undergraduate students trained to conduct the survey. All calls were made on Tuesday through Friday to eliminate problems related to different media use levels between weekdays and weekends. Thus, reports of "yesterday" activities refer to weekdays in this study.

A minimum number of five attempts were made to contact busy, no-answer, and machine-answered numbers. Eliminating 109 ineligible numbers (businesses, nonworking numbers, disconnects, faxes, etc.) of the 705 numbers contacted,[1] the survey completion rate was 56% (333 completed interviews out of 596 eligible numbers). Overall, there were 110 unreachable numbers (no answer, busy, answering machine) and 153 refusals. The final sample of 333 had 181 digital subscribers (54.4%) and 152 nondigital subscribers (45.6%).

Dependent Variables

The research instrument used yielded two dependent variables on which this study focused: early adopters and adoptive innovativeness.

Early adopters. Because the system's digital cable penetration rate was about 14% when this study was conducted, the digital subscribers included in this study fell into the early adopters category of Rogers's (1995) five adopter types. Disconnectors (i.e., former digital subscribers currently subscribing to analog cable service) were excluded from the analysis because their characteristics may be different from those of original nondigital subscribers.

Adoptive innovativeness. In addition to the simple distinction as to whether a respondent was a digital subscriber or an analog-only subscriber, a second dependent variable was used in this study: adoptive innovativeness. This dependent variable was operationally measured by obtaining respondent answers to the question "How long have you been a digital cable subscriber?" The response range was 1 (*nondigital subscriber;* 46% of the sample), 2 (*less than 1 year;* 40.2% of the sample), 3 (*1 year to less than 18 months;* 12% of the sample), and 4 (*over 18 months;* 1.8% of the sample). Thus, this dependent variable measures the speed of consumer adoption with respect to digital cable.

Independent Variables

Demographics. To acquire demographic data, respondents were asked about their age, income, level of education, and number of children age 18 or under. Ratio scales were used for age (years) and for number of children living at home; ordinal scales were used to measure income, ranging from 1 (*less than*

---

[1]The remaining phone numbers (45 for digital subscribers, 50 for nonsubscribers) were never contacted due to the limited availability of the Michigan State University Telephone Research Laboratory for this study (only 2 weeks).

$10,000) to 6 (*over $120,000*) and education, ranging from 1 (*no high school education*) to 6 (*graduate or beyond college education*).

Media use.   TV viewing time was measured by respondent self-reports of the amount of viewing in the morning, afternoon, and evening on the previous day with the following questions. "Yesterday morning before noon [yesterday afternoon from noon to 7 p.m.; yesterday evening from 7 p.m. to 12 midnight], how much time did you watch television?" Responses to the three day parts were measured separately and summed to create the composite measure—overall TV viewing time. In addition, respondents were asked to report the frequency with which they read a newspaper ("How many days did you read a newspaper last week?") and their frequency of moviegoing ("About how many times did you go to see a movie in a theater during the last 3 months?").

Technology ownership.   Respondent subscribership to premium cable channels (e.g., HBO) was treated as a dummy variable (0 = *don't have;* 1 = *have the channels*). For measuring technology ownership, respondents were asked whether they owned any of a list of five electronic devices: a video camera, a VCR, a video game system, a CD player, and a personal computer. Each type of technology ownership was then dummy coded (0 = *none;* 1 = *own*). The number of items owned was then summed to reflect the extent of each respondent's technology ownership.

Innovative attitudes.   Respondents' attitudes about the innovativeness of themselves and their cable company were measured by asking the following question: "On a scale of 1 to 10 where 1 means *not technically progressive at all,* or low tech, and 10 means *very technically progressive,* or high tech, how would you rate yourself (your cable company)?"

Satisfaction.   Cable service satisfaction was measured by asking how satisfied respondents were with three service dimensions: customer service, quality of programs, and variety of programs (e.g., "How satisfied are you with customer services such as repair, ordering, or billing issues?"). A 4-point Likert scale ranging from 1 (*very satisfied*) to 4 (*very dissatisfied*) was used for each question. After coding was reversed (i.e., very satisfied respondent scores were recoded from 1 to 4, etc.), the satisfaction scores were summed (Cronbach's α = .73).

Data Analysis

To test the study's hypotheses with respect to early adopters, a discriminant analysis was performed because the dependent variable is a categorical variable. The analysis yields a group mean for each variable with a statistical level of significance (Klecka, 1980). In addition, a hierarchical multiple regression analysis with hierarchical entry of predictor variables was performed to assess the relative influence of the independent variables in predicting respondent adoptive innovativeness. Before conducting the regression analysis on the second dependent variable, Pearson correlation coefficients were computed among all independent variables to screen for potential multicollinearity problems. The highest intercorrelation among the independent variables was .41, suggesting that serious multicollinearity problems probably did not exist with respect to the estimated regression model.

RESULTS

Sample Profile

The sample was 47.7% men and 52.3% women. The mean age of the sample was 39.3 and the median household income category was $30,000 to $60,000. When compared with the most recent U.S. Bureau of the Census (1996) data in which the median age was 34, the median household income was $32,264 (1994), and there were 51.2% women, the composition of the sample was not very different from that of the national population, except for education. In this sample, the average respondent was relatively better educated compared to the United States as a whole (80.9% of this sample had at least some college education compared with only 47.7% in the national population).

Discriminant Analysis—Early Adopters Results

The item means and F values produced by discriminant analysis are presented in Table 1. In conducting discriminant analysis, prior probabilities were set at .5 because the probability of being a subscriber or a nonsubscriber was equal. Missing data in the discriminating variables were replaced with the item mean. The overall analysis was significant, $\chi^2(13, N = 333) = 102.81, p < .001$. The canonical correlation was .57 (33% explained variance), and Wilks's Lambda was .67. Group centroids were located at .587 (subscribers) and –.825 (nonsubscribers). As shown in Table 2, the discriminant model correctly classified 74.5% of the cases, a 24.5% improvement over chance.

Contrary to expectations, no demographic variables were found to have a significant impact on whether respondents chose to subscribe to digital cable. In other words, digital subscribers were not significantly different from nonsubscribers in terms of age, income, education, and number of children. Thus, H1 was not supported.

TABLE 1
Discriminant Analysis: Digital Cable Subscribers Versus Nonsubscribers

		Means		
Variable	Unstandardized Coefficients	Subscribers	Nonsubscribers	F
Age	.00	36.7	38.5	0.98
Income	.16	3.4	3.3	0.40
Education	-.25	4.7	4.9	2.14
No. of children	-.16	0.6	0.7	0.95
TV Viewing[a]	.10	10.4	8.8	11.63*
Radio	.05	4.4	4.2	0.26
Newspaper	-.04	4.9	5.2	0.53
Moviegoing	.07	3.1	2.5	2.90
Premium subscribership	.84	0.7	0.4	25.40**
Media ownership[b]	.14	3.7	3.5	2.80
Attitude (self)	.16	7.4	6.3	23.96**
Attiitude (company)	.39	7.9	6.4	54.01**
Satisfaction	.11	3.3	2.9	18.56**

Note.   Wilk'sΛ = .67,χ^2(13, N = 333) = 102.81, p < .001.

[a]Total TV viewing reflects the sum of viewing during morning, afternoon, and evening. [b]The index reflects an average ownership of personal computers, video cameras, video game systems, CD players, and VCRs.

*p < .05. **p < .001.

TABLE 2
Classification Results of Discriminant Analysis

		Predicted Group Membership			
		Subscriber		Nonsubscriber	
Actual Group	N	%	No.	%	No.
Subscriber	181	80.7	146	19.3	35
Nonsubscriber	152	32.9	50	67.1	102

Note.   Percent of grouped cases correctly classified = 74.5.

With respect to media use, early digital cable subscribers were found to spend significantly more time watching television than nonsubscribers (p < .05). However, other media use variables such as radio listening, newspaper reading, and moviegoing revealed no significant differences between digital subscribers and nonsubscribers. Thus, H2 was only partly supported.

There were more premium channel subscribers in the digital group than in the analog-only group (p < .001), which supported H3. However, H4 was not supported, suggesting that digital subscribers do not have more technical devices than nonsubscribers.

With regard to innovative attitudes, digital cable subscribers were significantly more likely to evaluate both themselves and their cable company as technologically progressive, relative to the group of nonsubscribers ($p < .001$). Thus, H5 and H6 were supported.

Finally, H7 was also supported, indicating that those who subscribe to digital cable are more likely to be satisfied with their current cable service ($p < .001$).

Hierarchical Regression—Adoptive Innovativeness Results

Table 3 provides the relative importance of individual variables in predicting adoptive innovativeness (i.e., the speed of consumer adoption) with respect to digital cable.

The regression model estimate yielded three significant predictors with respect to adoptive innovativeness: respondents' attitude toward the innovativeness of their cable company ($\beta = .29$), respondents' television use ($\beta = .25$), and respondents' subscribership to premium channels ($\beta = .17$). The findings suggest that consumers who perceive their cable company to be tech-

TABLE 3
Hierarchical Multiple Regression: Predictors of Adoptive Innovativeness

Predictors	Step Entered	R	R^2	R^2 Change	β
Demographics	1	.15	.02	.02	
Age					−.01
Income					.08
Education					−.05
No. of children					−.11
Media use	2	.32	.10	.08**	
Television					.25**
Radio					.04
Newspaper					−.02
Moviegoing					.11
Media ownership	3	.41	.17	.07**	
Premium subscribership					.17*
Media ownership					.11
Attitude	4	.52	.27	.10**	
Toward self					.07
Toward company					.29**
Satisfaction					.03

Note. Step 1, $F(4, 261) = 1.461$, $p = .21$; Step 2, $F(8, 257) = 3.777$, $p < .001$; Step 3, $F(10, 255) = 5.187$, $p < .001$; final model, $R = .52$, $R^2 = .27$, $F(13, 252) = 7.271$, $p < .001$.
    *$p < .05$. **$p < .001$.

nologically progressive, who watch more television, and who subscribe to one or more premium channels will adopt digital cable service earlier than other consumers. Surprisingly, however, no demographic variables made a significant contribution to the variance explained. A total of 27% of the variance was explained after all of the predictor variables were entered into the regression equation.

DISCUSSION

In this study, I profiled early digital cable subscribers by comparing digital subscribers to nonsubscribers in terms of demographics, media use, media ownership, innovative attitudes, and satisfaction with existing cable service. The findings generally support hypotheses derived from diffusion theory and from earlier empirical studies, which have attempted to empirically test diffusion theory's application to cable industry product innovation. The primary exception in this study is that no demographic factors were found to have a significant impact on consumer adoption (i.e., age, income, education level, and number of children). In particular, because income is considered to be one of the most important factors in the early stage of diffusion of innovations, the finding that income was not related to digital cable subscription is unusual. As Umphrey (1991) noted, cost is an important factor in determining whether current cable customers choose to upgrade, downgrade, or maintain their current level of cable service. Perhaps because the initial cost to upgrade to digital cable is approximately $50 ($40 for installation plus a $10 monthly fee), respondent income is less relevant as a decision factor with respect to digital cable subscriptions. It is also possible that other factors such as customer attitudes or satisfaction with cable may dominate cost relative to income level as a factor, as indicated in a previous study (Jacobs, 1995).

As for the consumption of other media, this study confirmed past findings that cable subscription is related to the amount of television consumers view (Greenberg et al., 1988; LaRose & Atkin, 1988b; Reagan, 1987). Digital cable subscribers watch significantly more television than nonsubscribers even in a media environment where a number of competing media exist and new media such as the Internet continue to emerge. Nevertheless, it is not clear whether heavy use of television leads to digital subscription or the subscription to digital cable stimulates more television viewing.

The results associated with other media uses were interesting. Consistent with cable companies' expectations, results of this study indicate a higher likelihood of digital cable subscription among those who subscribe to premium channels. There is clearly more discontinuity in moving from basic-only subscription to digital subscription than in going from premium subscription to digital. Benefits for the premium subscribers who upgrade to digital cable (e.g., multiplexed movie channels) are larger than for basic-only upgraders. As a result, earlier adoption of digital cable among premium subscribers compared with basic subscribers is to be expected. This finding suggests that the cable companies' strategy of targeting premium subscribers can be expected to be successful in the early stages of digital cable deployment. However, in view of the fact that a significant number of nonpremium subscribers also subscribe to digital cable, cable marketers must not ignore the benefits of marketing digital cable to this group in addition to premium subscribers.

The most interesting study result emerged from respondents' self-reported attitude toward the innovativeness of their cable company. Respondents who perceived their company to be technologically progressive were more likely to have upgraded to digital cable service. This suggests that a cable company may be able to increase service upgrades among its current subscribers, all other things equal, by promoting itself as technologically innovative, especially during new product introductions.

In this study, once again the importance of a good relation between a cable company and its subscribers was found to be significant. The study clearly indicates that digital subscribers were more satisfied than were nondigital subscribers, all other things equal. Although it is possible that digital subscriber satisfaction is higher as a result of becoming digital subscribers, it is more likely that digital subscribers were already more satisfied with cable service prior to subscribing to digital service. This is based on their higher use of other cable services, as reported here and in previous research (Jacobs, 1995; LaRose & Atkin, 1988a).

In terms of theoretical contributions, the results of this study lend support to the theory that demographic variables are of less importance in trying to explain cable subscribership. Albarran and Umphrey (1994) argued that demographic factors are "less useful in predicting [cable] subscribership" (p. 56), as did Jeffres and Atkin (1996) who further suggested that "a new set of attitudinal variables to supplement demographics ... be considered" (p. 328).

The results of this study also have implications for cable marketers. First, this study suggests that cable companies should position digital service as an innovative service, valuable to those who love television, and which offers important benefits to premium channel subscribers. Second, it may be useful to market digital as a subcategory of a more comprehensive marketing campaign designed to promote the local cable company as technologically innovative. Early adopters of innovative technologies appear to be likely to purchase new technologies from companies they view as high tech and technologically progressive. As cable operators continue to roll out new products (e.g., high-speed cable modems, etc.), this type of marketing campaign is likely to prove beneficial particularly given the increasingly competitive environment faced by cable operators.

Limitations and Future Research

As already noted, the sample used in the study was from a single market. Likewise, the composition of the sample was slightly different from the U.S. population. Furthermore, the sample of digital subscribers analyzed here may have been influenced by the marketing appeals used by this market's local cable company and by the nature of the service itself. Another limitation is that I assumed in this study that the digital subscribers included in the sample upgraded from analog cable service. However, this was not actually verified in the survey. Some respondents could be new to cable and actually have begun cable service with digital cable.

This study utilized a limited number of predictive variables, which accounted for only 27% of the total variance explaining digital cable adoption. Future research should include more potential predictors such as individual lifestyle or psychographic variables to provide a fuller explanation of the factors accounting for digital cable adoption. In addition, regarding the anticipated impacts of digital cable on users' behaviors, future study is encouraged to determine how new cable products (e.g., NVOD, SVOD, VOD, etc.) influence consumer demand with respect to competing methods of video and film delivery such as video rentals and moviegoing.

ACKNOWLEDGMENTS

This research was supported by the Hallym Academy of Sciences at Hallym University, Korea, 2002–1.

I would like to thank Thomas Baldwin, Stephen Lacy, and three anonymous reviewers for their valuable comments on an earlier version of this article.

REFERENCES

Albarran, A. B., & Umphrey, D. (1994). Marketing cable and pay cable services: Impact of ethnicity, viewing motivations, and program types. *Journal of Media Economics, 7*(3), 47–58.

Atkin, D. J., Jeffres, L. W., & Neuendorf, K. A. (1998). Understanding Internet adoption as telecommunications behavior. *Journal of Broadcasting & Electronic Media, 42,* 475–490.

Atkin, D., & LaRose, R. (1994a). A meta analysis of the information services adoption literature: Lessons to be learned from cable and telephony. In J. Hanson (Ed.), *Advances in telematics* (pp. 91–110). Norwood, NJ: Ablex.

Atkin, D., & LaRose, R. (1994b). Profiling call-in poll users. *Journal of Broadcasting & Electronic Media, 38,* 217–227.

Baldwin, T. F., McVoy, D. S., & Steinfield, C. (1996). *Convergence: Integrating media, information and communication.* Thousand Oaks, CA: Sage.

Bruce, I. (1996, August). *Early adoption of DBS: Information, attitudes and early adoption.* Paper presented at the Association for Education in Journalism and Mass Communication, Anaheim, CA.

Collins, J., Reagan, J., & Abel, J. D. (1983). Predicting cable subscribership: Local factors. *Journal of Broadcasting, 27*(2), 177–183.

Colman, P. (1998, May 4). Digital cable: When, not if. *Broadcasting & Cable,* 42–46.

Danko, W. D., & MacLachlan, J. M. (1983). Research to accelerate the diffusion of a new invention. *Journal of Advertising Research, 23*(3), 39–42.

Dickerson, M. E., & Gentry, J. W. (1983). Characteristics of adopters and non-adopters of home computers. *Journal of Consumer Research, 10,* 225–235.

Dupagne, M. (1999). Exploring the characteristics of potential high-definition television adopters. *Journal of Media Economics, 12,* 35–50.

Ettema, J. S. (1984). Three phases in the creation of information inequities: An empirical assessment of a prototype videotex system. *Journal of Broadcasting & Electronic Media, 30,* 325–329.

Ettema, J. S. (1989). Interactive electronic text in the United States: Can videotex ever go home again? In J. Salvaggio & J. Bryant (Eds.), *Media use in the information age* (pp. 105–123). Hillsdale, NJ: Lawrence Erlbaum Associates, Inc.

Greenberg, B. S., Heeter, C., D'Alessio, D., & Sipes, S. (1988). Cable and noncable viewing style comparisons. In C. Heeter & B. S. Greenberg (Eds.), *Cableviewing* (pp. 207–225). Norwood, NJ: Ablex.

Haring, B. (1997, November 17). Why cable firms love digital TV. *USA Today,* sec. 7, p. 1.

Higgins, J. M. (1997, December 1). Cable nets do digital. *Broadcasting & Cable,* p. 6.

Higgins, J. M. (2000, May 1). Top 25 cable operators. *Broadcasting & Cable,* 24–50.

Jacobs, R. (1995). Exploring the determinants of cable television subscriber satisfaction. *Journal of Broadcasting & Electronic Media, 39,* 262–274.

Jacobs, R. (1996). Cable television subscribers: A comparison of complainers and noncomplainers. *Journal of Media Economics, 9*(3), 37–49.

Jeffres, L., & Atkin, D. (1996). Predicting use of technologies for communications and consumer needs. *Journal of Broadcasting & Electronic Media, 40,* 318–330.

Katz, R., & Peers, M. (1998, November 30). Digital cable plexs muscle. *Variety,* pp. 19–22.

Klecka, W. R. (1980). *Discriminant analysis.* Beverly Hills, CA: Sage.

LaRose, R., & Atkin, D. (1988a). Satisfaction, demographic, and media environment predictors of cable subscription. *Journal of Broadcasting & Electronic Media, 32,* 403–413.

LaRose, R., & Atkin, D. (1988b). Understanding cable subscribership as telecommunications behavior. *Telematics and Informatics, 5,* 377–388.

LaRose, R., & Atkin, D. (1992). Audiotext and the reinvention of the telephone as a mass medium. *Journalism Quarterly, 69,* 413–421.

Lin, C. A. (1998). Exploring personal computer adoption dynamics. *Journal of Broadcasting & Electronic Media, 42,* 95–112.

McAdams, D. (1999, August 23). Dancing into digital. *Broadcasting & Cable,* 28–32.

Ostlund, L. E. (1974). Perceived innovation attributes as predictor of innovativeness. *Journal of Consumer Research, 1,* 23–29.

Paul Kagan Associates, Inc. (1999). *Cable TV financial databook* (p. 10). New York: Author.

Petrozzello, D. (1997, December 15). Image boost, choices key to 'cablenet.' *Broadcasting & Cable,* p. 105.

Reagan, J. (1987). Classifying adopters and nonadopters of four technologies using political activity, media use and demographic variables. *Telematics and Informatics, 4*(1), 3–16.

Reagan, J., Ducey, R. V., & Bernstein, J. (1985). Local predictors of basic and pay cable subscribership. *Journalism Quarterly, 62,* 397–400.

Robertson, T. S. (1967). The process of innovation and diffusion of innovation. *Journal of Marketing, 31,* 14–19.

Rogers, E. M. (1995). *Diffusion of innovations* (4th ed.). New York: Free Press.

Umphrey, D. (1991). Consumer costs: A determinant in upgrading or downgrading of cable services. *Journalism Quarterly, 68,* 698–708.

U.S. Bureau of the Census. (1996). *Statistical abstract of the United States.* Washington, DC: Author.

Williams, F., Strover, S., & Grant, A. U. (1994). Social aspects of new media technologies. In J. Bryant and D. Zillmann (Eds.), *Media effects advances in theory and research* (pp. 463–482). Hillsdale, NJ: Lawrence Erlbaum Associates, Inc.

JOURNAL OF MEDIA ECONOMICS, *15*(3), 209–225

The Economics of Video On Demand: A Simulation Analysis

Ronald J. Rizzuto
Reiman School of Finance
Daniels College of Business
University of Denver

Michael O. Wirth
Department of Mass Communications and Journalism Studies
School of Communication
University of Denver

Simulation analysis and sensitivity analysis are used to identify the factors most likely to determine whether video on demand (VOD; i.e., movies on demand) is economically viable. The impact of subscription video on demand (SVOD) and of time-shifted, on-demand services on VOD economics is also explored. VOD movie buy rates, Hollywood and cable operator revenue splits, and VOD peak utilization rates are identified as key economic viability factors. SVOD and/or time-shifted services could also contribute positively to VOD economics if significant buy rates can be achieved without major impacts on peak utilization rates.

"VOD [video on demand] is a Holy Grail ... for many in the cable industry, having been pursued, thought about and championed for more than two decades" (Ellis, 2001, p. V-2). In spite of many tests, significant technological advancement, and repeated predictions that movies on demand[1] or VOD is just around the corner, VOD service was still only available to a small percentage of cable subscribers in 2001 (0.9 million VOD homes in 2001 vs. 0.2 million in 2000; *K Book: The Guide to Broadband Stats and Standings,* 2001, 2002). However, the 450% increase in

---

Requests for reprints should be sent to Ronald J. Rizzuto, Reiman School of Finance, Daniels College of Business, University of Denver, Denver, CO 80210. E-mail: rrizzuto@du.edu

[1]Movies on demand is a service whereby individually selected real-time movies are delivered on a movie-by-movie basis from a cable headend into the homes of subscribers who pay a fee for each movie selected.

VOD homes that occurred during 2001 has many predicting that 2002 will be the year that VOD finally begins to live up to its potential (see, e.g., Applebaum, 2001b; *K Book*, 2001, 2002; Lafferty, 2002; *MediaWeek*, 2001). On the other hand, others have been skeptical that VOD will reach critical mass in 2002 (Baumgartner, 2002), if at all (Donahue, 2001).

For VOD to live up to its "killer application" potential (Brister, 2001), it will have to deliver a return on investment for cable entrepreneurs. "Operators have learned one lesson from the billions of dollars incinerated in the financial fantasy of the Internet ... to spend money on products only when revenues are in clear sight" (Grotticelli & Kerschbaumer, 2001, p. 34).

As a result, in this article we take an arm's length look at the economics of VOD by examining the following research questions:

- What factors are likely to be most important in determining whether VOD is economically viable?
- How is the economic viability of VOD likely to be affected by subscription video on demand (SVOD) and time-shifted broadcast or cable program on-demand services?

To obtain an answer to these research questions, in the next section we provide a brief history of VOD. A discussion of VOD technology follows, along with a description of the methodology used to analyze the research questions. We then present the basic VOD economic simulation model along with the base case assumptions used in the analysis. Next, we present the results of our simulation and sensitivity analyses followed by conclusions.

BRIEF HISTORY OF VOD

As mentioned earlier, until very recently (Ellis, 2001), commercial VOD had only been available to a handful of consumers via a number of market tests including Viewer-Controlled Cable Television, the TCI, AT&T, and U.S. West VOD test in Littleton, Colorado, which began in 1992 (Allen, Heltai, Koenig, Snow, & Watson, 1993); Full Service Network, the Time Warner Cable VOD test in Orlando, Florida, which began in 1994 (Collette, 2000); Command Performance, the 1994 Southern New England Telephone VOD test in Connecticut (Baldwin, McVoy, & Steinfield, 1996); and Your Choice TV, the on-demand video program replay test managed by the Discovery Channel, which began in 1992 (Collette, 2000). Although these VOD tests were popular with consumers (see, e.g., Rozansky, 1997), "true video on demand was too expensive" (Rath, Wanigasekara-Mohotti, Wendorf, & Verma, 1997, p. 72). As a result, cable operators (as well as cable's direct broadcast satellite [DBS] competitors) began to deploy near video on demand (NVOD), which devotes multiple channels to deliver each month's most popular movies (e.g., devoting four channels to a 2-hour movie means the movie would start every 30 min; devoting eight channels to a 2-hour movie would allow the movie to start every 15 min), simulating video on demand at a fraction of the cost (Ellis, 2001).

More recently, the costs of commercially deploying VOD have declined, and cable operators have spent "more than 50 billion dollars ... upgrading their networks" (Brister, 2001, p. 5F) and deploying digital cable to approximately 16 million subscribers (Applebaum, 2001a). As a result, cable multiple system operators have begun to roll out VOD in a number of commercial test markets in the hope that actual market results will merit broad VOD deployment in the near future. For example, some of the approximately 36 VOD deployments (Sweeting, 2001) that were in place by year-end 2001 included Charter Communications in St. Louis, Missouri, Los Angeles, Atlanta, Georgia, and Fort Worth, Texas (Iler, 2001); Insight Communications in Rockford, Illinois, Columbus, Ohio, Evansville, Indiana, and Anderson, Indiana (Iler, 2001); Cablevision Systems in Long Island ("Cablevision bows," 2001); Time Warner Cable in Tampa Bay/St. Petersburg, Florida, Honolulu, Hawaii, Austin, Texas (Grotticelli & Kerschbaumer, 2001) and Columbia, South Carolina, which is testing SVOD (Nye, 2001); AT&T Broadband in Atlanta, Georgia, and Los Angeles (Smith, 2001); Comcast in Philadelphia, Baltimore, and Sarasota, Florida ("Comcast is offering VOD," 2001; "Cox and Comcast spend millions," 2001); Cox in San Diego, California, and Hampton Roads, Virginia (Grotticelli & Kerschbaumer, 2001); and Adelphia with an SVOD test in northern Ohio (F. O. Williams, 2001). Going forward, Baumgartner (2002) predicted that "cable operators will offer VOD in 100 to 120 markets by the end of 2002" (p. 17).

In addition to VOD (i.e., movies on demand), cable entrepreneurs hope to develop significant additional on demand revenue streams. The most talked about services to date include (a) an SVOD service that provides premium channel subscribers with on-demand access to the monthly programming being provided by premium channels to which they subscribe (Brown, 2002; Kerver, 2001), (b) a time-shifted broadcast or cable program on-demand service allowing "subscribers [to] view previously-broadcast [or cablecast] content on demand" (Shapiro, 2001, p. 3), and (c) a targeted advertising service allowing advertisers to use VOD technology to reach digital subscribers with individually targeted advertisements (Brady, 2001). The simulation and sensitivity analyses we provide assess the impact on VOD profitability of adding SVOD and time-shifted broadcast or cable program on-demand services.

VOD TECHNOLOGY

To a consumer, VOD appears to be a relatively simplistic operation. Consumers simply call up a menu on the TV screen, select the desired on-demand programming by depressing a button on the remote control, wait a few seconds, and begin watching the selected program. VOD also gives consumers the ability to pause, rewind, and fast-forward as if they were watching the program on a VCR, a DVD, or a personal video recorder (PVR). However, what appears simple to the consumer is very complicated technologically. Because a basic understanding of how VOD works from a technological perspective is critical to understanding the economics of VOD, a brief description of VOD technology is provided following.

When the consumer calls up the menu, the program guide is either called up from within the digital set-top box (STB) or downloaded into the STB from the headend. Once the consumer makes a selection, the information is sent to the appropriate application server via the cable return path. There are usually several application servers, one for each application (e.g., movies on demand, sports on demand, news on demand, etc.). The application server, which is responsible for certifying subscriber authorization levels and issuing server output requests, then communicates with the server manager, the video servers, the system resource or bandwidth manager, and the subscriber management system. The server manager manages the video servers by setting up and tearing down sessions between the video servers and the STB.

Video servers, the main component of the VOD system, store and manage VOD content as well as deliver the content via the downstream network to the STB. The video servers "packetize" the content, and a laser converts the content to light beams for transport from the headend to the hybrid fiber coax node. The light waves are converted to radio frequency signals at the node and transported via coaxial cable to the subscriber's home. The digital STB then reassembles, decompresses, and decodes the packets, and the consumer begins to watch the selected on-demand program.

The storage capacity required (represented as the number of streams) will vary depending on the number of titles offered, the number of digital cable subscribers, and peak utilization (i.e., the highest number of simultaneous users allowed by the system architecture). Typically, each 100-min movie that has been digitally compressed using Motion Picture Experts Group (MPEG) 2 compression requires approximately 1.7 gigabits (Gb) of digital storage space.[2] Each MPEG-2 video stream requires approximately 3.85 megabits per sec (Mbps) of bandwidth. Hence, if a cable node serves 1,000 cable subscribers, 20% of them subscribe to digital cable, and VOD peak utilization is 10%, the node would need 20 video streams of capacity (i.e., $1,000 \times 20\% \times 10\%$).[3] The number of 6-MHz channels that a cable operator devotes to VOD is a function of the modulation scheme (i.e., the method of

---

[2]An uncompressed 100-min movie requires approximately 70 Gb of storage capacity.

[3]Time Warner's Full Service Network made a significant contribution to VOD economics by finding that the VOD peak utilization rate was just under 10%, not 25% as had been projected prior to the Full Service Network experiment (Schley, 2000).

imprinting information onto a communication carrier) used by the operator. If an operator uses 256-QAM (quadrature amplitude modulation), 10 video streams (i.e., 10×3.85 Mbps = 38.5 Mbps) can be digitally compressed into a 6 MHz analog channel (Q. Williams, 1999). So, delivering the 20 video streams in the preceding example requires two 6-MHz channels.

The system resource or bandwidth manager allocates video streams to different channels and generates reports about bandwidth usage. The subscriber management system manages the subscriber account information, applies spending limit or parental control restrictions, and collects the subscriber's purchase history. This subscriber billing information is then interfaced with the cable operator's subscriber billing system.

An *asset manager* or *content director* is a software system that manages the content on the video server. This includes adding and removing content. Integrated video server/management software suite VOD systems are currently distributed to cable operators by four primary vendors: Concurrent Computer Corporation, Diva Systems Corporation, nCube, and SeaChange International. They also support both centralized (i.e., all video servers are located at the headend) and distributed (i.e., the video servers are located throughout a system in hubs serving 20,000 homes) VOD systems.

METHOD

"Simulation is the manipulation of a symbolic, analogical or iconic model to determine the changes in one or more dependent variables induced by changes in one or more independent variables" (Wentz, 1972, p. 451). The analyses provided herein utilize a symbolic simulation model (i.e., a model using mathematical equations) to examine the economics of VOD.

In the next section, we detail the variables and variable values included in our base case VOD simulation analysis. A sensitivity analysis follows in which the values of key independent variables are changed one at a time from the base case to assess the impact of key individual variables on VOD profitability.

Because of the limitations of sensitivity analysis,[4] a grand simulation analysis (i.e., Monte Carlo simulation) also is included to provide a more robust assessment of VOD profitability. This tool allows consideration of all possible outcomes by enabling simultaneous inspection of the entire distribution of possible variable values. In the grand simulation analyses (see Table 1), a range of values was specified

---

[4]When faced with great uncertainty, the fundamental limitations of sensitivity analysis include (a) the impossibility of exploring the entire range of possible outcomes and (b) the single-point estimates of profitability provided by sensitivity analysis do not indicate the likelihood of achieving an overall profitable outcome.

TABLE 1
VOD Economic Sensitivity and Grand Simulation Analyses

VOD Sensitivity Analysis Scenarios	Net Present Value (in Millions)	Internal Rate of Return (%)
1. VBC (i.e., movies on demand only)		
A. VBC (buy rate = 2; program cost = 55%)	1.96	24
B. Buy rate = 1; program cost = 55%	−2.25	2
C. Buy rate = 2; program cost = 70%	−1.36	8
D. Buy rate = 1; program cost = 70%	−3.91	−11
E. 20% peak utilization (vs. 10% in BC 1A)	−5.19	1
2. VBC + SVOD		
A. VBC + SVBC (50% buy rate; $3.95/month)	3.71	31
B. Low SVOD case – 20% buy rate; $3.95/month	2.66	27
C. High SVOD case – 100% buy rate; $3.95/month	5.46	38
D. VBC + SVBC with 20% peak utilization	−3.44	6
3. VBC + SVBC + time shifted		
A. VBC + SVBC + time shifted (100% buy rate)	4.95	36
B. Low time-shifted case (25% buy rate)	3.96	32
C. High time-shifted case (400% buy rate)	8.65	51
D. VBC + SVBC + time-shifted BC (with 20% peak utilization)	−2.20	9
Grand simulation analyses (integrating all scenarios)		
1. Results with 1,000 iterations (i.e., trials)[a]	3.97	27
2. Results with 10% to 30% peak utilization (1,000 iterations)	.41	16

Note.   VOD = video on demand; BC = base case; VBC = VODBC; SVOD = subscription VOD; SVBC = SVODBC.

[a]All variable values are input simultaneously using a uniform distribution. Assumptions were (a) peak utilization varied between 10% and 20%, (b) movie buy rate varied between 1 and 3, (c) SVOD buy rate varied between 0% and 100%, (d) SVOD retail rate varied between $3.00 and $6.95, (e) time shifted buy rates varied between 0% and 400%, and (f) movie program costs varied between 55% and 70%.

for six key variables: peak utilization (10% to 20%), movie buy rates (1–3), SVOD buy rates (0% to 100%), SVOD retail rate ($3.00 to $6.95), time-shifted program buy rates (0% to 400%), and movie programming costs (55% to 70%). The range of each variable was entered as a uniform distribution, allowing for an equal probability of occurrence for each value within the range (e.g., a 10% peak utilization rate is just as likely as a 10.5% or a 20% rate). Alternative distributions (i.e., normal, triangular, Poisson, etc.) that weight the outcomes differently could have been utilized; however, we did not have enough information to justify the selection of one of these distributions.

The Microsoft Excel™ add-in program Crystal Ball (Decisioneering, 2000) was utilized to perform the grand simulation analyses. This program generates various cash flows and net present values by rearranging the combinations of input values. Theoretically, thousands of combinations of values give rise to thousands of combinations of cash flows and net present values. However, a sample of 1,000 iterations usually provides a good indication of the relevant range of outcomes. As a result, the grand simulation results provided are based on 1,000 iterations.

BASE CASE VOD ECONOMIC SIMULATION MODEL

A number of general assumptions underlie our VOD (i.e., movies on demand) economic simulation model. First, the model utilizes the standard finance definition of free cash flow (FCF) as its determinant of VOD costs–benefits. That is, $FCF = (R - C - D)(1 - t) + D - \Delta WC - CX$, where

FCF = free cash flow
R = revenue
C = operating costs
t = tax rate
D = depreciation
ΔWC = working capital investment (set = 0 in our model)
CX = capital expenditures

Second, our VOD economic model treats the cable operator's investment in digital set-top converters and channel capacity as a sunk cost because (a) most U.S. cable operators invested in digital set tops as a defense against DBS competition as well as to expand channel capacity and offerings,[5] and (b) VOD technology, cost structures, and infrastructure were not yet viable at the time most operators made their digital STB deployment decisions. Third, because most operators have already upgraded their bandwidth to 750 MHz or more, the channel capacity used for VOD delivery is considered to be a sunk cost. As a result, the analysis that follows focuses on the incremental free cash flow and risks associated with VOD deployment on an already upgraded two-way digital platform.

Base Case Capital Costs

The fixed capital components for a VOD system include video servers, an application server, a subscriber management system and billing software, a server manager, a system resource or bandwidth manager, and an asset manager or content director. In addition to this VOD hardware and software, a cable operator must also invest capital to purchase modulation equipment and to remodel the headend to ac-

---

[5]If a cable operator has not yet invested in digital STBs, then it would be appropriate to consider the capital costs of the digital set top in any VOD economic analysis. In fact, in this situation a cable operator would want to consider the economics of digital video with and without VOD deployment.

commodate VOD equipment. VOD capital costs vary by system size but generally break down as 54% for VOD hardware and software and 46% for modulation equipment and remodeling costs.

Capital costs per stream are typically used as a common denominator for representing VOD capital costs. Our VOD base case simulation's capital cost per stream is estimated to be $825 (VOD server, $300 per stream; software, $150 per stream; modulation and transport, $275 per stream; and remodel costs, $100 per stream; Shapiro, 2001).[6] The number of streams that a system requires is a function of the digital customer base as well as of the estimated peak utilization rate. For example, if a system had 100,000 digital customers and estimated a 10% peak utilization rate, it would need to build a 10,000-stream VOD system (i.e., peak utilization rate × number of digital customers). At a cost of $825 per stream, the total capital costs would be $8.25 million.

In deciding on a VOD deployment strategy, a cable operator must consider the cable system's existing NVOD offerings and its video storage capacity.

As noted previously, most operators who are deploying VOD have already launched digital video services including a suite of pay-per-view (PPV) channels devoted to NVOD service with movie start times at 15-min, 30-min, or 60-min intervals. NVOD is used for newly released movies into the PPV distribution window, approximately 45 days after they have been released to video stores. Frequently, a cable operator has more than 20 digital channels devoted to NVOD. The more channels currently devoted to NVOD, the greater the likelihood that a VOD service offering (i.e., movies on demand) will choose to concentrate on the latest top releases (movies just released for VOD distribution but, it is hoped, not yet available for NVOD distribution), recent favorites (the more popular movies in the current NVOD window), and classic movies (see SeaChange International, 2001).

The other key decision with respect to a cable operator's VOD strategy is the number of titles to offer. The greater the number of titles offered, the greater the required investment in storage capacity. In addition, although the number of titles will drive buy rates, it will also have an impact on peak utilization rates. In theory, the greater the product offering the higher the peak utilization rate and the greater the number of video streams required.

VOD economics depend critically on the scale of the investment. The more titles offered and the more streams provided the greater the investment required. A large-scale investment strategy is riskier than a small-scale investment because the fixed capital investment in storage and video stream capacity has to be made up front before market acceptance and product buy rates are known.

---

[6]Our base case simulation adds $100 per stream for headend remodeling costs to Shapiro's (2001) estimated VOD capital costs per stream of $725.

Base Case Revenues

In the base case VOD model discussed following, we patterned the scale of the investment after the typical U.S. cable system VOD launch model in which the VOD movie library consists of approximately 100 movie titles (made up of the latest top releases, recent favorites, classics, and adult movies), and the system is built for a 10% peak utilization rate. Typically, the 100 movies are priced similar to Time Warner of Austin's iCONTROL Library: new releases, $3.95; classic and recent favorites not available on existing PPV, $1.95; and adult movies, $6.95 (SeaChange International, 2001).

Anticipated VOD movie buy rates vary considerably. At the upper extreme, some cable operators theorize that consumers, who on average rent approximately three movies per month, will eliminate all three video store rentals and replace them with three VOD buys per month. This theory is supported by a number of perceived VOD benefits over video stores: the convenience of never being out of stock of the top 10 movies; the convenience of ordering from one's living room; and elimination of video store late fees, which have been estimated by various security analysts to represent 30% of Blockbuster Video's revenues.

Although VOD may ultimately replace video store rentals, changes in consumer behavior will take time to evolve. As a result, our base case simulation model assumes two VOD purchases per month with 80% of those purchases being top 10 new release movies, 15% adult movies, and 5% classic and recent favorite movies. This results in a $4.30 weighted average price for our base case VOD system. We present the sensitivity of VOD economics to different buy rates in the next section.

The pricing and buy rates for SVOD are even harder to estimate due to limited experience with this product. Each of the major premium programmers (HBO, Showtime, and Starz Encore) developed and tested SVOD during 2001 (Baumgartner & Lafferty, 2000; Umstead, 2001). Both the concept of SVOD and various pricing models have been tested. Adelphia's initial SVOD test was as a free, value-added service included as part of a premium subscription (Moss, 2001). Other cable operators have tried several pricing schemes. Mike LaJoie, Time Warner Cable's Vice President of Corporate Development, indicated that systems are getting significant buy rates from all three price points they are testing ($3.95, $6.95, and $9.95) for HBO's SVOD service (LaJoie, 2001). Our base case simulation uses a 0% buy rate for SVOD. The sensitivity analysis we provide in the next section utilizes various SVOD buy rates to determine SVOD's potential impact on VOD profitability.

Research regarding the demand and pricing of on-demand, time-shifted broadcast or cable programs is currently in its infancy. Several programmers (Arts & Entertainment, ESPN, Comedy Central, Cartoon Network, and Discovery) are beginning to test this concept and possible pricing strategies. However, given the emergence of PVRs, there is significant concern with respect to both the pricing and viability of on-demand service. Shapiro's (2001) VOD economic model estimated buy rates for this time-shifted service between 0% and 800% (i.e., eight buys per month). In his research, Shapiro estimated a price of $1 per program. In our base case simulation model we assume a 0% buy rate. In our sensitivity analysis buy rates are varied to estimate the impact of an on-demand, time-shifted program service on VOD profitability.

Base Case Operating Costs

The major operating expense item for VOD is movie programming costs. This expense item, along with the quality of programming (i.e., the release window), is a major factor in the overall long-term success of VOD. Hollywood studios are beginning to reach agreements with the cable industry on the pricing and availability of top release movies for VOD. The terms of the agreements have not been disclosed. The current revenue splits for PPV and NVOD are 50% for Hollywood, 5% for IN Demand, and 45% for the cable operator. As a result, our base case simulation utilized a 55% programming cost for movies. However, the sensitivity analysis considered movie programming costs up to 70% of revenue.

Programming costs for SVOD are currently minimal because premium programmers' strategy for launching this service has been to reinforce and support the demand for their core premium services. Eventually programmers will start charging for SVOD. As a result, the SVOD scenarios provided in our sensitivity analysis utilized a cost of 50% of revenue for SVOD programming. For time-shifted programming costs, we used the same revenue splits used for movies (55% programmers, 45% cable operators). Although these costs may be less, no empirical information exists for projecting a lower value.

Other base case operating costs include (a) VOD marketing costs estimated at 5% of revenues and approximately equal to cable's historical marketing cost average of 4% to 5% of revenues; (b) VOD salary expense estimated to be one employee for every 3,000 streams at an average annual salary of $60,000 plus benefits, equal to 25% of annual salary (i.e., $15,000) and projected to increase 4% per year; (c) VOD hardware maintenance costs estimated to be 6% of total capital invested (historically, cable system maintenance costs have averaged approximately 6% of capital invested); and (d) VOD bad debt expense estimated to be equal to the historical bad debt percentage in cable operators' core video business, or 2% of revenues.

Base Case Profitability (Free Cash Flow)

Table 2 provides a brief summary of the key assumptions, revenues, costs, and measures of profitability for the base case VOD simulation model for a cable sys-

TABLE 2
Base Case Video on Demand Profitability (Free Cash Flow)
Simulation Model

Summary Financials	Year[a]				
	0	1	2	3	10
Movie revenue		3406	5108	8514	8514
Total other revenues		0	0	0	0
Total revenues		3406	5108	8514	8514
Costs					
Total programming costs		1873	2810	4683	4683
Total other operating costs		633	922	1248	1325
Total costs		2506	3732	5930	6007
Operating cash flow		899	1377	2584	2507
Depreciation		389	861	1199	121
Earnings before tax		510	516	1385	2386
Taxes (38%)		194	196	526	907
Net income		316	320	859	1479
Depreciation		389	861	1199	121
After tax cash flow		705	1181	2057	1600
Capital expenditures	2723	1361	2723	0	0
Free cash flow	−2723	−656	−1542	2057	1600
Cumulative free cash flow	−2723	−3378	−4920	−2863	9823
Net present value ($r = 15\%$)	1960.40				
Internal rate of return (%)	24				
Payback (years)	4.41				

Note. Key assumptions were the following: Basic customers = 165,000; homes passed = 300,000; movie buy rates = 2 buys per month; average price per movie = $4.30; movie programming costs = 55% of revenue; digital customers = 33,000 to 82,500 (i.e., digital penetration increasing from 20% to 50%); capital costs = $6,806,250 (8,250 video on demand streams [10% of 82,500] at $825 per stream).

[a]Summary financials in thousands of dollars.

tem passing 300,000 households with 165,000 basic customers. A more detailed description of the base case model is provided in the Appendix.

The base case simulation model assumes that the cable system has a digital penetration of 20% (33,000 customers) during the 1st year of VOD deployment and that digital penetration will grow to 50% by year 3 and remain constant through year 10.

The base case return on investment (i.e., the internal rate of return) on the $6.81 million investment in VOD is 24%, the net present value (with a 15% cost of capital) is $1.96 million, and the payback period is 4.4 years. Thus, our base case simulation measures of profitability indicate that VOD is a profitable investment because most cable operators would fund projects with internal rates of return greater than 15% to 20%.

This base case model may be viewed by some as conservative because (a) it does not include any SVOD or time-shifted program revenue; (b) VOD operating costs are higher than for the core cable video business (i.e., the VOD base case cash flow margin—operating cash flow and revenue—of approximately 30% is much lower than the 40% margin typical of the core video business); and (c) the model does not include any value beyond the 10th year (i.e., no terminal value is included).

On the other hand, some may view the base case simulation model as aggressive (a) because it assumes two video purchases per month per customer or $8.60 in VOD revenue per customer per month, and (b) because VOD programming costs may turn out to be greater than 55% of revenue.

VOD SENSITIVITY AND GRAND SIMULATION RESULTS

To test the sensitivity of VOD economic outcomes to changes in key variable values, a range of more conservative to less conservative assumptions (from the base case simulation) was used to assess VOD profitability. Table 1 presents the results from three sensitivity analysis scenarios: the base case scenario, the base case scenario plus SVOD, and the base case scenario plus both SVOD and time-shifted programming. Each of the scenarios considers several cases in which key variable values are varied from the base case. In addition to the sensitivity analysis, the results from two grand simulation analyses are provided in Table 1.

Scenario 1—VOD Base Case

As noted previously, the VOD base case simulation utilized a buy rate of two movies per month and a revenue split between Hollywood and cable operators of 55% and 45%, respectively. As the results provided in Table 1, Scenario 1, illustrate, both of these assumptions are critical to the economics of VOD. If consumers purchase only one movie per month (holding all other values constant), the net present value drops to –$2.25 million (Scenario 1B). Likewise, if the buy rate remained at two movies per month, but VOD program costs (i.e., Hollywood's share of VOD revenues) increase to 70%, the net present value declines to –$1.36 million (Scenario 1C). Thus, a miscalculation of either of these variables will have a significant negative impact on the profitability of the movies on demand VOD model. Recent articles surrounding the announcement of a VOD licensing agreement between IN Demand and DreamWorks SKG included speculation that the revenue split was 60% DreamWorks, 5% IN Demand, and 35% cable operators. This 65% cost, with a two movies per month buy rate scenario, translates into a net present value of –$254 thousand and a 14% internal rate of return.

Scenario 1E underscores the importance of the peak utilization decision. If a cable operator builds its system for a VOD peak utilization of 20%, but peak market demand is on average only 10%, this excess capacity reduces the net present value from $1.96 million to –$5.19 million. Cable operators can mitigate the risk of overestimating peak demand by initially building for a low peak utilization and then scaling up their systems' VOD streaming capacity as demand increases. For example, Cox initially engineered its San Diego, California, system for a peak utilization of 7% but has planned to increase its VOD streaming capacity as peak demand approaches peak capacity (Cole, 2001). Cox engineered its system so that it could increase its streaming capacity on either a system-wide or node-by-node basis.

Scenario 2: VOD Base Case + SVOD

The cable system in the SVOD scenarios was assumed to have an 80% premium service penetration among its digital subscribers. Therefore, the 82,500 digital subscribers in the model (in years 3 through 10) purchased 66,000 premium subscriptions. Some may buy multiple premium services and others may buy none (i.e., our focus is on premium units not premium households). An SVOD buy rate of 50% (as used in the SVOD Base Case in Table 1) means that 33,000 SVOD subscriptions were sold to digital subscribers. Also, the SVOD scenarios presented here did not forecast any secondary impacts from SVOD such as increased digital premium subscriptions or decreased churn rates (for premium services, digital cable, etc.).

Our sensitivity analysis results (see Table 1) suggest that SVOD significantly enhances the movies on demand VOD model. The net present value of the VOD investment increased from a base case value of $1.96 million (Scenario 1A) to $3.71 million (Scenario 2A) when SVOD, with a 50% buy rate at a $3.95 monthly price point, was incorporated into the VOD simulation equation.

Scenarios 2B and 2C (see Table 1) show the impact of different buy rates on VOD–SVOD economics. A 20% buy rate (vs. a 50% buy rate) reduced the net present value from $3.71 million to $2.66 million, a 28% reduction. If the SVOD buy rate is 100%, net present value increased to $5.46 million.

Scenario 2D in Table 2 underscores the importance of the interrelation between SVOD buy rates and peak utilization. If SVOD increased VOD revenue and did not significantly increase peak utilization, SVOD dramatically increased overall VOD profitability (i.e., net present value increased from $1.96 million to $3.71 million). However, if SVOD (at its base case values) doubled the VOD streaming capacity required to satisfy peak VOD demand, cable operators' overall VOD net present value became negative (–$3.44 million).

Scenario 3: VOD Base Case + SVOD Base Case + Time-Shifted Programming

Time-shifted broadcast and basic cable network programming potentially enhance the economics of VOD and SVOD. If consumers prefer the convenience of an on-demand order versus the premeditated recording of a PVR, an additional revenue stream could be added to the VOD economic model.

The Scenario 3 results provided in Table 1 indicate that the incremental profitability impact of time-shifted broadcast and cable programming is $1.24 million (i.e., the net present value of VOD and SVOD increased from $3.71 million to $4.95 million) if all digital subscribers purchased one time-shifted program per month at a retail price of $1. However, if the average subscriber purchased one time-shifted program only once every 4 months (i.e., a 25% buy rate), the incremental impact was minimal, that is, net present value increased by only $0.25 million to $3.96 million (Scenario 3B). Alternatively, if the average digital subscriber made four time-shifted buys per month, the net present value exploded to $8.65 million (Scenario 3C) as long as peak utilization remains 10%.[7]

Finally, Scenario 3D underscores the importance of peak utilization with respect to the economic viability of the time-shifted program revenue stream. If the peak utilization rate increased from 10% to 20% as a result of digital subscribers' purchasing one time-shifted program per month in addition to their VOD and SVOD purchases, the net present value of the combined VOD enterprise (i.e., VOD base case + SVOD base case + time-shifted base case) dropped from $3.71 million to –$2.2 million.

Grand Simulation Analysis

The results for Grand Simulation 1 provided in Table 1 indicate the most likely net present value and internal rate of return across the range of values provided for the six key variables included in the analysis. After 1,000 trials, Grand Simulation 1 estimated a likely net present value of $3.97 million and an internal rate of return of 27%. (Rerunning Grand Simulation 1 for 2,000 trials left the net present value [$3.98 million] and internal rate of return [27%] essentially unchanged.)

The primary limitation of simulation analyses is that they are highly dependent on being able to correctly specify the range of variable outcomes and the appropriate probability of each outcome. As a result, we decided to rerun the simulation with an expanded range for the peak utilization rate (due to the critical nature of this variable with respect to both capital costs and capacity for adding additional VOD revenue streams at the margin). Grand Simulation 2 in Table 2 indicates that VOD remains a profitable investment for cable entrepreneurs when the range of peak utilization rates was expanded to 10% to 30% (from 10% to 20%). However, the net present value fell to $0.41 million (from $3.97 million).

CONCLUSION

The analysis provided in this article underscores the importance of three key VOD factors: movie buy rates, Hollywood and cable operator revenue splits, and peak

---

[7]If time-shifted buy rates reach 800% as Shapiro (2001) speculated, the net present value is $13.6 million with 10% peak utilization and $6.45 million with a peak utilization rate of 20%.

utilization rates. If any of these factors deviate significantly from their expected base case values (e.g., if monthly buy rate = 1, programming costs = 60% or more, or peak utilization = 20%), the VOD economic model is in jeopardy. The risks represented by these key factors can be mitigated, at least to some extent, if significant SVOD and/or time-shifted broadcast or cable program buy rates are achieved.

In the future, the VOD economic model could be altered by several factors. On the positive side, new developments in storage and processing costs could dramatically reduce VOD costs per stream. Likewise, positive consumer experiences with on-demand television could dramatically accelerate the rate of evolution from a broadcast to an on-demand video delivery model. On the negative side, if Hollywood is successful with its plans to deliver VOD via the Internet (Lyman, 2001), it could decide to bypass VOD via digital cable. Likewise, increased penetration of PVRs could reduce the market for cable-delivered VOD.

In sum, the rollout and experience with VOD in the United States are still in their infancy. If VOD begins to move up the adoption curve (i.e., the product life cycle), the VOD economic model will continue to evolve.

ACKNOWLEDGMENT

We gratefully acknowledge the assistance provided by Diane Burkhardt of the University of Denver's Westminster Law Library, Lisa Backman of The Cable Center's Barco Library, and Greg DePrez of Starz Encore in completing this article.

REFERENCES

Allen, J. R., Heltai, B. L., Koenig, A. H., Snow, D. F., & Watson, J. R. (1993, January/February). VCTV: A video-on-demand market test. *AT&T Technical Journal, 72,* 7–14.

Applebaum, S. (2001a, December 10). Technology '01 review: A new wave of services. *Cablevision,* p. 16.

Applebaum, S. (2001b, December 10). Technology '02 preview: More good stuff on the way. *Cablevision,* p. 17.

Baldwin, T. F., McVoy, D. S., & Steinfield, C. (1996). *Convergence: Integrating media, information & communication.* Thousand Oaks, CA: Sage.

Baumgartner, J. (2002, January 1). Critical mass for VOD? Not yet. *CED, 28,* 17.

Baumgartner, J., & Lafferty, M. (2000, July). Vendors put VOD on front burner. *CED, 26,* 28–40.

Brady, S. (2001, November 26). Concurrent pitches targeted ads at show. *Cableworld,* p. 56.

Brister, K. (2001, September 26). Video on demand: Hollywood puts cable operators on hold over licensing fees. *The Atlanta Journal and Constitution,* p. 5F.

Brown, R. (2002, January 16). I want my SVOD. *TV Guide Online.* Retrieved January 18, 2002, from http://www.tvguide.com/techguide

Cablevision bows ambitious digital service. (2001, November 1). *CED, 27,* 20.

Cole, A. (2001, February). Deployment showcase: Cox rolls out VOD in San Diego, readies for nation-wide launch. *Communications Technology, 18,* 74–83.

Collette, L. (2000). Pay television services. In A. Grant & J. Meadows (Eds.), *Communication technology update* (7th ed., pp. 19–29). Boston: Focal Press.

Comcast is offering VOD in 3 counties starting today. (2001, December 11). *The Baltimore Sun,* p. 2C.

Cox and Comcast spend millions in systems upgrade. (2001, June 22). *The Associated Press State & Local Wire.* Retrieved July 26, 2001, from http://www.lexis.nexis.com/universe

Decisioneering. (2000). *Crystal Ball 2000 users manual.* Denver, CO: Author.

Donahue, A. (2001, December 31). VOD still vaporous. *Video Business,* p. 38.

Ellis, L. (2001). *Definitive broadband.* Littleton, CO: Genuine Article Press.

Grotticelli, M., & Kerschbaumer, K. (2001, July 9). Slow and steady. *Broadcasting & Cable,* pp. 32–42.

Iler, D. (2001, August 6). VOD shining brightly in cable universe. *Broadband Week,* p. 18.

K book: The guide to broadband stats and standings. (2001, Fall). New York: Media Central/Primedia.

K book: The guide to broadband stats and standings. (2002, Winter). New York: Media Central/Primedia.

Kerver, T. (2001, November 12). What's next for cable? *Cablevision,* pp. 16–23.

Lafferty, M. (2002, January 1). Which comes first? ITV or VOD? *CED, 28,* p. 12.

LaJoie, M. (2001, November 26). Comments at CTAM pre-Western Show Conference. *CableFax,* p. 1.

Lyman, R. (2001, August 17). Hollywood moves to rent movies online. *The New York Times.* Retrieved August 19, 2001, from http://www.nytimes.com

MediaWeek (2001, February 21). New York: Credit Suisse First Boston, p. 3.

Moss, L. (2001, June 11). Video-on-demand is here—Now who's going to pick up the tab? *Cableworld.* Retrieved June 16, 2001, from http://www.inside.com

Nye, D. (2001, June 21). Time Warner to add HBO video-on-demand to digital cable in Columbia, S.C. *The State.* Retrieved July 26, 2001, from http://www.lexis.nexis.com/universe

Rath, K., Wanigasekara-Mohotti, D., Wendorf, R., & Verma, D. (1997, June). Interactive digital video networks: Lessons from a commercial deployment. *IEEE Communications Magazine, 35,* 70–74.

Rozansky, M. L. (1997, May 7). Time Warner is pulling the plug on ambitious interactive television project. *The Philadelphia Inquirer.* Retrieved July 26, 2001, from www.lexis.nexis.com/ universe

Schley, S. (2000). *Fast forward.* Littleton, CO: Genuine Article Press.

SeaChange International. (2001). Texans get an early taste of video-on-demand. Case study, Time Warner Cable of Austin. Retrieved January 10, 2002, from www.seachangeinternational.com

Shapiro, D. S. (2001, February 27). Tech tutorial: VOD. *Broadband brief.* New York: Bank of America Securities.

Smith, J. (2001, December 31). Video on demand awaits economic upturn. *Rocky Mountain News,* p. 1B.

Sweeting, P. (2001, December 17). NCTA puts VOD homes at 6 million. *Video Business,* p. 50.

Umstead, R. T. (2001, June 11). HBO to launch SVOD in South Carolina. *Multichannel News,* p. 177.

Wentz, W. B. (1972). *Marketing research: Management and methods.* New York: Harper & Row.

Williams, F. O. (2001, December 2). Coming next at Adelphia: Movies on demand. *The Buffalo News,* p. B11.

Williams, Q. (1999, December). Evaluating VOD deployment options: Molding technology to meet subscriber's needs. *CED, 25,* 92–96.

APPENDIX
VOD—Base Case Simulation Model Assumptions

Variable	Year			
	1	*2*	*3*	*10*
Passings	300,000	300,000	300,000	300,000
Basic penetration	0.55	0.55	0.55	0.55
Basic customers	165,000	165,000	165,000	165,000
Digital penetration	0.2	0.3	0.5	0.5
Digital customers	33,000	49,500	82,500	82,500
Peak utilization	0.1	0.1	0.1	0.1
Number of VOD streams	3,300	4,950	8,250	8,250
Cost per VOD stream	$825	$825	$825	$825
Buy rates movies	2	2	2	2
Top release movie price	$3.95	$3.95	$3.95	$3.95
Classic movie price	$1.95	$1.95	$1.95	$1.95
Adult movie price	$6.95	$6.95	$6.95	$6.95
Top release movie (% of buys)	80	80	80	80
Classic movie (% of buys)	5	5	5	5
Adult Movie (% of buys)	15	15	15	15
Average price per movie	$4.30	$4.30	$4.30	$4.30
Digital premium penetration (%)	80	80	80	80
Digital premium customers	26,400	39,600	66,000	66,000
SVOD buy rates (penetration)	0.00	0.00	0.00	0.00
SVOD monthly rate	$3.95	$3.95	$3.95	$3.95
Time-shifted broadcast buy rates	0	0	0	0
Time-shifted broadcast rates	$1.00	$1.00	$1.00	$1.00
Movie programming costs	0.55	0.55	0.55	0.55
SVOD programming costs	0.50	0.50	0.50	0.50
Time-shifted programming costs	0.55	0.55	0.55	0.55
Maintenance costs (% of invested capital)	0.06	0.06	0.06	0.06
Employees (headcount)	2	2	3	3
Annual salary and benefits	$75,000	$78,000	$81,120	$106,748
Bad debt expense (% of revenue)	0.02	0.02	0.02	0.02
Marketing expense (% of revenue)	0.05	0.05	0.05	0.05

Note. VOD = video on demand; SVOD = subscription video on demand. The income tax rate was 38% and depreciation was calculated using 7-year life, Modified Accelerated Cost Recovery System depreciation.

www.ingramcontent.com/pod-product-compliance
Ingram Content Group UK Ltd.
Pitfield, Milton Keynes, MK11 3LW, UK
UKHW020427010325
455677UK00029B/1041